EXPLORING TRANSSEXUALISM

EXPLORING
TRANSSEXUALISM

Colette Chiland

Translated by David Alcorn

Published in English in 2005 by
H. Karnac (Books) Ltd.
6 Pembroke Buildings, London NW10 6RE

© Presses Universitaires de France, 2003
French Edition *Le transsexualisme* published in 2003

English translation © Colette Chiland, 2004

British Library Cataloguing in Publication Data

A C.I.P. for this book is available from the British Library

ISBN 1 85575 332 4

www.karnacbooks.com

Contents

Introduction

Everybody is talking about it, but who really knows what it is all about? Even today transsexualism remains an enigma. The media make no attempt to clarify the complex issues that underlie the question: shades of meaning and doubt do not make audience ratings rise. All sorts of rash declarations are made, such as: "nowadays a man can be changed into a woman, a woman into a man". The plain truth is that only appearances are changed – plus, where the law of a given country permits it, civil status; the individual is granted the possibility of living as a man or as a woman, as a member of the opposite sex, the sex opposite to the one he or she was assigned at birth, the sex which remains that of his or her body (according to our present knowledge).

This leads on to fundamental questions such as: What is a man? What is a woman? Society does not grant the same status to men and to women. But in transsexualism, social condition is not the issue, *identity* is. Does one's sex define one's identity? Some have invented a distinction between sex and gender, thereby making it possible to talk of "gender identity". What is sex? What irresistible force compels some people to reject their sex? How can they want – whatever the cost – to "change their sex"? And "whatever the cost" indeed implies that of a significant mutilation that puts the person's health – and perhaps even life – at risk; all that, without realizing that what is being sought after is basically impossible.

This book is not the fruit of simple speculation and *a priori* ideas. I am consulted by and listen to people who want a physician to transform their bodies with the help of hormones and of surgery. They phrase their request in a disturbing manner: "I want you give me back my *true* body, the one that corresponds to my sense of identity"; for them, stitches all over their body would still be preferable to this despicable penis or these hated breasts. The acme of eroticism for some is the ultimate horror for others.

Transsexuals do have certain things in common, which is why we use the one term to describe them all. Yet each one of them is different from all the others; each has followed his or her own path in life, and we have to be attentive to what each of them has to say that is different from what we may already have heard.

Supposing it were true that this man, who is every inch a man, is, somewhere inside himself, a woman? Not in his external genital organs, not in his gonads (testicles), not in his hormones, not in his prostate gland, not in his chromosomes, not in the fact that he has no developed breasts, uterus or ovaries – but in his brain. Supposing this were some form of intersex condition, someone who combines male and female biological characteristics, that as yet we have proved unable to detect?

Supposing it were true that this woman is partly a man, a man without a penis, testicles, a prostate gland, a beard, a man with a uterus, ovaries and breasts? A man inside her brain, in a way that is difficult to prove, not only while she is alive but even after her death.

What are we to think of studies that not only propose this kind of hypothesis but even, basing their argument on animal models which can hardly apply to questions of gender identity, claim that it is practically proven?

At any rate, the path that leads to transsexualism begins very early on in life, whether the reason is biological or psychological and inter-actional, or both. Why should biological aetiology be proof of innocence, while its psychological and interactional counterpart gives rise to guilt feelings? At what point in life would it still be possible to change the path that the person is following? Is there no other way out but the scalpel and the syringe? Can whatever is in the mind be changed?

Chapter One

Transsexualism: what's new?

I t would seem that there have always been people, men and women, who reject their original sex and wish to live as members of the opposite sex. What is new is the term "transsexualism", as is the offer that some physicians make to "reassign" a person's sex. The way in which contemporary society comes to terms with the condition is new, as is the train of ideas it brings in its wake.

I. The word itself

It is an easy matter to put a date on the word itself. It developed in three stages.

Firstly, in 1923, Magnus Hirschfeld, a German sexologist, used it occasionally in the form *seelischer Transsexualismus* (transsexualism of the soul or mental transsexualism) when referring to the intersexed. Then, in 1949, D. O. Cauldwell wrote a paper with the title "Psychopathia transexualis" in which he described a case that we would nowadays call female-to-male transsexualism. Finally, in 1953, Harry Benjamin coined the word *transsexualism*, a term that in the space of ten years or so would establish itself as the correct designation for a highly specific condition, different from transvestism or eonism.

The word brings to mind the idea of crossing a frontier between the sexes: in 1963, Georgina Turtle wrote a book with the title *Over the Sex Border*. It comes close also to the idea of transgression: an infringement of the established order of things as decreed by nature, by God or by human law, which holds that the distinction between the two sexes is of crucial importance.

II. A medical offer

Benjamin, who established the term in its final form, argued also that psychotherapy is powerless in cases of transsexualism; the only possible treatment is hormone administration and surgery. That point of view prevailed throughout the past 50 years. That medical offer was followed immediately by a tremendous upsurge in demand. In 1953, the year in which the word "transsexualism" was coined, three clinicians, Christian Hamburger, Georg K. Stürup and Erling Dahl-Iversen, published a report on the procedures they had used to treat George Jorgenson, who became Christine Jorgenson. This was not the first time a hormonal-and-surgical transformation had been attempted, but it was at that point the most successful (no attempt was made to create a vagina in Jorgenson's first operations) – firstly because the patient survived the operation and secondly because he-then-she managed to "pass as" a woman by adopting a career as a music-hall artiste. In that one year, Hamburger received 465 letters from people who saw themselves in the story of George-who-became-Christine and were asking for the same treatment .

Is the prescription of opposite-sex hormones and surgical procedures a "cure"? Do they lead to "recovery"? The situation is a highly paradoxical one: healthy organs are removed and the patient has to keep on taking substitutive hormones; nothing has been changed as regards the patient's feelings of discrepancy between the sex as proclaimed by the body and that as experienced in his or her soul. It can only be a palliative measure, enabling the patient to live better; outcome studies of patients who have undergone "hormonal and surgical sex reassignment" are of major importance in showing that patients do indeed have a better life afterwards.

The practice of hormonal and surgical sex reassignment is what distinguishes the contemporary phenomenon of transsexualism from the situation prevalent in other cultures, in which the experience of rejecting one's given sex is similar, though the response of society is different. Developments in scientific and medical knowledge and technique – in particular in endocrinology and plastic surgery [Hausman 1995] – have made possible a "transformation" that elsewhere and in the past was hoped for yet remained unattainable until recently.

The Hijras or eunuchs in India come to mind. For the past thousand or so years, they – principally men but there are also some women – have lived as a community. They practise a home-made form of emasculation that sometimes leads to death (surgery is not permitted under Indian law). They are devotees of the fearsome mother goddess Bahuchara Mata. They have renounced all personal fertility, believing that they have the power to bless others so that the latter might have children. Without necessarily being invited, they come to give blessings and to dance their comical routines whenever a baby boy is born, or attend weddings where they play out scenes centred on the boundless and aggressive aspects of female sexuality. They arouse some negative feelings, especially as regards their activity as prostitutes.

The North American Indian Berdaches are an institution that is well-nigh extinct. They too were mainly males, though there were a few females too. They wore women's clothes, or clothes that were in some other way distinctive. A Berdache was neither man nor woman, but a kind of third gender fulfiling the role of shaman. Their status, therefore, was quite prestigious.

Among the Inuit, Bernard Saladin d'Anglure has described a third, social, sex: the *sipiniit* children, who were supposed to have changed their sex at birth (though there are also a certain number of intersexed among the Inuit). The mother has a part to play in ascribing this status – the dreams she has during her pregnancy and her fantasies are what lead to her decision. There is also the fact that, in Inuit culture, it is important to have children of both sexes – here, in other words, the atom of kinship consists of brother, sister and the parental couple and not only, as for Lévi-Strauss [1973], of a son and the parental couple. This situation is a very peculiar one, because, at adolescence, the child is reassigned to his or her biological sex, a predicament that is not easy to cope with. The child, considered to be in communication with supernatural forces, often becomes a shaman; when a male *sipiniit* reaches adulthood, he tends to marry a woman who has had, *mutatis mutandis*, the same experience in life.

In our own culture, there are those whom I call the "anonymous of the past", those who managed to live incognito as members of the opposite sex, the discovery being made only after their death. Had hormonal and surgical sex reassignment existed then, they would probably have had recourse to it. Their fate was personal and individual, just as in the case of today's transsexuals, not attributed by some other person and shaped by cultural considerations.

III. Transsexualism as a culture-specific phenomenon

Transsexualism with hormonal and surgical sex reassignment is a feature of our contemporary culture not only because nowadays science and technology make the procedure possible but also because of the place that the individual occupies in present-day society. Much is demanded of the individual: to acquire knowledge that is always being refined, to master techniques that are constantly being developed, to be capable of taking the initiative. Tradition is no longer what determines learning or *mores*. "God is dead" – there are still believers, of course, and people who practise their faith. The needs that recognized faiths met still exist: the need for supernatural intervention in order to put up with the difficulties of the human condition, the powerlessness that one experiences *in fine* when faced with illness, old age, death. These needs are met also by the various religious sects, clairvoyants, and healers of all sorts. But the individual person is no longer supported by a network of beliefs and rules, though obviously there are laws which, on a great number of issues, govern the relationships between people; that said, as far as one's private life is concerned, individuals have to invent their own code of conduct, their own "ethics".

The result is that individuals are nowadays demanding rights that were hitherto unheard of in any society; this goes hand in hand with a decrease in the acknowledgement by the individual of his or her obligations towards others. "Since what I am asking for its technically possible, since it brings me pleasure, then I am entitled to obtain it". On this topic, Denis Salas [1994] makes some interesting comments.

Public opinion is not unanimous. Some will defend traditional values; some are fundamentalists; there are various groups for the defence of some right or other; there are lobbies. At their most spontaneous, some show sympathy; others are shocked. Most people make judgements without being properly informed. Those who do try to enquire and to think have a difficult task ahead of them. This book is intended to be a contribution to that quest for information and effort to reflect.

Chapter Two

From the intersexed to transsexuals

T hough a new word may not have been coined as regards the intersexed, a new meaning was given to an old word thanks to their condition: "gender".

I. John Money and the invention of gender

John Money was a psychologist in the world's first paediatric endocrinology unit, set up by Lawson Wilkins at the famous Johns Hopkins Hospital in Baltimore. Children from all over the United States – and many from elsewhere – who presented intersexed conditions were seen in this unit.

These children may or may not manifest some degree of ambiguity as to their external genitalia, but they do possess a mixture of male and female characteristics such that it is difficult to know what sex should be attributed to them. Nowadays the problem is better understood than in the 1950s and we have new means of investigation at our disposal (karyotyping, improved hormonal measures, laparoscopy, etc.) that enable us, if not to give a simple answer, at least to frame the question in much more comprehensive terms.

From time to time in the past, the problem was discovered only at puberty, when sexual development did not follow the expected path as laid down by the child's assigned sex.

In all societies, an infant is assigned to one or other of the recognized sexes, male or female – legal texts say masculine and feminine – usually on the basis of the appearance of the external genitalia. In some societies there are recognized special cases. Among the Inuit, as we have seen, some children are said to have changed sex at birth and are raised as members of the opposite sex from that indicated by their genital organs; in adolescence, however, this situation becomes complicated when these *sipiniit* children revert to their biological sex.

The appearance of the genital organs may be misleading, as in the case of androgen insensitivity syndrome, in which the sex organs (external genitalia) seem to be female, in spite of an XY chromosome formula and the presence of androgens. In the absence of any indication that other cases of this type exist or have existed in the family, the child will be declared to be a girl, without any hint that something may be inappropriate, since the external genitalia appear quite unambiguously to be those of a girl.

There exists also a quite extraordinary syndrome known as steroid 5-α reductase occurring at birth, which changes with adolescence when the appearance of the genitals changes from female to male; this is a hereditary syndrome that Julianne Imperato-McGinley has studied in the Dominican Republic, where it is called *guevedoche*, "penis at age 12". It can also be found in New Guinea.

The appearance of the genital organs may be ambiguous: a big clitoris with impalpable testicles could be mistaken for a hypospadiac penis in which the urethral meatus is not in the normal position, as in the case of congenital adrenal hyperplasia in a baby with XX chromosomes, a uterus and ovaries. Some of these children have been raised as girls, others as boys.

The significant discovery made by John Money, together with John and Joan Hampson, was that, in their vast majority, children with identical biological make-up experience themselves as belonging to the sex in which they have been raised (100 out of 105 in one of their samples).

John Money introduced the idea of gender in 1955, when he spoke of "gender role". According to him, it was Evelyn Hooker who, in an exchange of correspondence with Money, first introduced the idea of "gender identity". The Los Angeles psychiatrist and psychoanalyst, Robert Jesse Stoller, adopted this differentiation between sex and gender, with "sex" being used to refer to a biological state and "gender" to a psycho-social condition. Indeed *Sex and Gender* was the title which he gave to two of his books [Stoller 1968, 1975]. He invented the idea of *core gender identity*, the feeling that one is male or female, which becomes firmly established towards the end of the second year or during the third year of life, while gender identity is the feeling of being masculine or feminine, which develops and diversifies throughout one's life. (Stoller does not use the term *role gender identity*, introduced by Ovesey and Person in 1973). Though Stoller is close to

Money on many issues, he attaches more importance than the latter does to biological forces; though he describes a particular pattern of psychological dynamics in families of those he calls "true transsexuals", he does not exclude the fact that a biological element may also be involved.

Sociologists and feminist groups seized on the term "gender", which as a result became increasingly popular. It then became deflected, however, and the emphasis began to be placed on its social aspects, to such an extent that the biological element was first forgotten and then called into question. Gender was presented as being a purely social distinction with no biological basis whatsoever. Having given considerable thought to the question, I feel that I have succeeded in understanding why it was possible to reach such an unreasonable conclusion. We perceive biological reality only through social representations that vary according to the prevailing period and culture – that much is true. However, even if its representations change, the fact remains that the body has always existed and that there is a difference between male and female, a difference that could be called the "sexual difference". Every society attempts to embroider on the perceptible and unchallengeable elements of that difference, and ends up by fabricating for men and women a destiny that nothing in the realm of nature can justify. It is quite legitimate to rebel against a social stereotype, without ignoring one's biological make-up. The sexual difference cannot be ignored; it is a distinctive feature of human beings to try to make meaningful that simple fact to which they can only submit.

II. How the intersexed are treated

In former times the intersexed were often considered to be monsters, not conforming to Nature's scheme of things or to the will of the gods; in other words as a deviation from the norm. Yet at the same time a "hermaphroditic ideal", to use Joyce McDougall's term [McDougall 1973 (1980)], is present in mythology and in the imagination of individuals. The division of human beings into two sexes is felt to be scandalous; none of us can embody the whole of humanity (sometimes it was even believed that men were the only true human beings – women were treated as a kind of by-product). When a child comes to realize that fact, the discovery is traumatic. The dream is being the other person while continuing to be oneself – of being both, in other words.

In Ancient Greece, children whose sex seemed doubtful at birth or appeared to change at puberty were left out in the open to die, or were drowned, or were burned alive; yet at the same time, according to Delcourt [1958 (1961)], the androgynous individual was in a highly elevated state of Nature and of godliness, and there was a god (though admittedly a minor one) called Hermaphroditus, represented in statue as a slender adolescent possessing the characteristics of both sexes, without any erotic component. The rites are those of cross-dressing, more often a male dressing up in female attire as a trick to ward off any hostile spirits in order to overcome the dangers that threaten a married couple as they have intercourse for the first time. Cross-dressing is a typical aspect of initiation rites, in which the boy dresses up in women's clothes, the more to assert his masculinity as he takes them off again. Delcourt [ibid.] adds that other ceremonies in which cross-dressing is practised by both sexes simultaneously and plays a significant role are suggestive of the idea of fertility rites. Dionysus, also a man-woman, a double being doubly powerful, was later, in the hellenistic era, represented as effeminate.

In Hinduism, Shiva sometimes appears united with his wife Parvati in the form of Ardhanishvara, part man (the right sagittal half) and part woman (the left sagittal half).

Some truly hermaphrodite animals do exist, either simultaneously like snails or successively like some fish and shrimps. A snail cannot fertilize itself; it has to mate with another. Fish and shrimp are fertile in each of their successive states; they are in turn wholly male and wholly female, the order of succession of the two sexes varying according to the species concerned.

There are no true hermaphrodites in the human species, however, even though sometimes we talk of hermaphrodites in order to distinguish them from pseudo-hermaphrodites. Hermaphrodites possess both testicular and ovarian tissue, either in separate gonads or in the form of ovotestes. Pseudo-hermaphrodites present different combinations of male and female biological components – for example, XY chromosome formula and female external genitalia, or ovaries and a big clitoris that could appear to be a penis.

Some have described this condition as an error of nature – as though Nature had a well-defined plan from which the individual concerned had deviated in the course of his or her development. Compared to an image of ideal development – in fact, that of a simple statistical majority – it is true to say that at certain moments development did not take place in the usual manner. But for such a person who tries to live with his or her body as it really is or as it will be after any attempted modification, the experience is that of "variation" as a human being rather than that of an aberration, of a teratological phenomenon; such persons long to be treated as human beings in their own right, even if they have to live with imperfect genital organs, sterility, etc.

In our culture the intersexed, under the influence of medical opinion, are considered to be living a tragic experience for which they are in no way responsible and which has nothing to do with their free will, while the evocation of possible psychological factors in the aetiology of transsexualism is felt by transsexuals as putting the burden of guilt on them, something that they vigorously reject. Yet nobody should feel any more guilty for something that occurred through interacting with the environment in early infancy than for some physical event that took place in one's body while *in utero*. Transsexuals insist on biological reasons for their problems, and have a strong tendency to call themselves intersexed – apparently allowing themselves in this way not to have to take a closer look at what goes on in their mind.

III. How the intersexed should be treated

The rules drawn up by John Money and his collaborators, especially the Hampsons and Anke Ehrhardt, lasted for almost half a century before being called into question more than had previously been the case as a result both of what happened to Joan-John [Colapinto 2000] and of the fact that intersexed patients, especially in the United States, began to set up self-help groups on an increasingly large scale.

Children feel themselves to belong to the sex in which their parents raise them, as long as they do so with conviction – that was the discovery Money made. It was therefore important, in order to support the parents' conviction and that of their child, that the genital organs be repaired as soon as possible in accordance with the child's assigned identity.

The chosen sex would be the one which, on balance, seemed more plausible given the state of the organ to be repaired. Constructing a penis is impossible, whereas creating a plausible vulva and vagina is within the bounds of possibility. A boy born without a penis was thus assigned to the female sex; though he would be sterile, he could pass for a woman. The appearance of the genital organs was more important than the chromosomal sex, for example.

If a mistake in the initial assignment was discovered later in life, the courts often corrected the person's civil status; this was not considered to be a change of sex but the correction of an error.

There are a number of problems with this approach.

A micropenis is not the same thing as no penis at all. The response to administration of androgens should be assessed in order to see if there is any possibility of further growth.

If an ordinarily masculinized boy loses his penis accidentally in the first months of life, is this comparable to the situation in which the penis does not develop normally? That happened to a boy called John: when he was seven months old, his penis was injured in the course of a clumsy attempt at circumcision; as a result, his twin brother was not circumcised. After some hesitation it was finally decided, on Money's advice, to amputate John's penis entirely, to remove his testicles and raise him as a girl, Joan. The parents seem to have done this quite convincingly. Money treats this case as a success – in his report, there are photographs of the child dressed as a girl – whereas in fact the child was increasingly unwilling to accept this feminization. In the end, at adolescence, his identity as a boy was restored to him, though he had neither penis nor testicles; he married a woman who already had three children, whom Joan-John raised. The documentary evidence presented by Colapinto shows that Money's behaviour was somewhat surprising and that the assessment was in fact marred by a lack of honesty. This case history calls into question the credit usually given to Money's reports.

A similar case has also been published [Bradley et al. 1998] which developed favourably in the direction of a female identity even though the person concerned had behaved in a masculine way in childhood and felt attracted to women. The question must therefore remain open.

Another problem is that of the reliability of parental conviction. Is it possible by stating the problem in all of its complexity to convince them to raise their child in a way contrary to that indicated by the chromosomal and gonadal sex? Or, as seems to have been Money's position, is it better simply to give them a rather vague explanation along the lines of incomplete and imperfect development? At present, since the law authorizes access to one's medical file and given the notion of informed consent, such vagueness would probably no longer be allowed. The contemporary view is that the parents should not be wilfully misinformed at the child's birth, nor should there be any prevarication towards the patient later on (whereas until recently access to one's medical file was refused).

The situation is a difficult one to cope with. Parents should have some form of psychological help. They cannot raise a child as if he or she were neuter; it is just as unbearable for them as it is for the rest of their circle of family and friends. A sex has to be ascribed to the infant, one of the two sexes that society recognizes, but at the same time leaving open another possibility for the future.

Milton Diamond, who has always opposed Money's theories, argues in favour of a moratorium. Until some serious research on the outcome of children who have been operated on early in life has been done, with the idea of encouraging informed decisions to be made, there should be no more surgical operations on children until they are old enough to take such a decision for themselves. This is also the position adopted by Anne Fausto-Sterling in her remarkably informative book *Sexing the Body* [2000].

For the past ten years or so a certain number of intersexed patients, now adults, have complained about the way in which they were treated. They had undergone several operations (shortening, burying or remodelling of the clitoris; attempts at repairing hypospadias; attempts at creating a vagina; ablation of gonads, etc.) which, they claim, diminished their erotic capacity and practically removed any hope of choosing to live as a member of the opposite sex. They have set up mutual support and assistance groups, the first of these being the one founded by Cheryl Chase in the United States, the *Intersex Society of North America*.

What these ex-patients have to say must be taken into consideration, even though, since all of the patients who have had such operations have not been interviewed, it is very difficult to estimate the percentage of those who are unhappy with their treatment compared to the entire sample. Those who are displeased make themselves heard, but we know nothing about those who are as satisfied as they can possibly be and remain silent.

Those who, like Joan-John, do not feel they belong to their assigned sex are afraid of being considered mad or treated as monsters until such time as sex reassignment becomes possible for them.

IV. Transsexuals

"Transsexuals" are defined as men or women who admit to having either a male or female sex organ but who claim that they do not feel they belong to their assigned sex. In other words, there is a contradiction between the sex of their body and that of their soul – or, to put it differently, between their sex and their gender. They are women imprisoned inside a male body, or men imprisoned inside a female one. If they consult a doctor they do so in order to have their "true body" restored to them. They do not feel themselves to be suffering from any mental disorder.

We could use the term "transsexuals" to refer to those who want hormonal and surgical sex reassignment and who express the trans-sexual theme in the way I have just described. A transsexual is someone who wants to cross the frontier between the sexes.

Some professionals would like to restrict the term "transsexuals" to those who have in fact undergone surgery. According to this view a transsexual is someone who has taken the plunge – but this runs counter to the wish of many transsexuals who, after the relevant oper-ation, want merely to blend in with the crowd of other men and women, to be simply a man or a woman and not to be looked upon as a transsexual.

With respect to candidates for hormonal and surgical sex reassign-ment, others make a distinction between true or primary transsexuals and secondary transsexuals, and agree to operate only on the former.

According to the definitions adopted by the international classifi-cation of diseases, no transsexuals evidence biological signs of being intersexed. We should add here: "in the present state of our knowledge and means of investigation".

So what exactly is this strange disorder? We see before us a man who looks every inch a man, whose medical record is normal for his assigned sex (external and internal genitalia, karyotype, hormone measurement, etc.), yet who says: "You see, it's obvious, isn't it, I'm a woman." And vice-versa when a woman, who looks just like a woman and whose medical analyses are normal for a woman, says: "You see, it's obvious, isn't it, I'm a man." Through time, thanks to wearing clothes typical of the opposite sex and to hormones, their appearance changes and begins more and more to resemble what they claim to be. But when we meet such patients for the first time we cannot but be puzzled.

The statement "Give me back my true body", and the belief that someone will be able to give them a real body of the opposite sex, are madness. I am using the word "madness" in a vague and colloquial manner; I am not saying "psychotic", a word that has a precise mean-ing in psychiatry. It is madness because it is impossible. Transsexuals have said to me: "You'll never make me believe that nobody can graft a penis or a uterus and ovaries, when kidney, liver and heart transplants are so commonplace ...". Let us suppose that one day we will indeed be able to do so. We could still quite legitimately think that it will never be possible to change the chromosomes or the whole of the inside of the body. At any rate, no-one has succeeded in doing so as yet.

To this mad request, physicians have responded with a mad offer. Patients were led to believe that a man would change into a woman because his penis was amputated, his skin folds were turned inside out so as to fabricate a vagina, he was castrated (ablation of the testicles), and his breasts began to develop thanks to the administration of oestrogens combined with mammary implants made out of silicone or some other material. Others were led to believe that a woman would become a man as if by magic thanks to mastectomy, hysterectomy and ovariectomy, and because facial hair began to grow and the voice broke thanks to the administration of androgens; phalloplasty would be used to fabricate something that would hardly even look like a penis, far less fulfil its functions.

The external appearance does change, of course. Surface criteria mean that one may look like, and be treated as, a woman or a man. A change in civil status may be possible. (This has been the case in France since 1992, when the final appellate court [Cour de Cassation] decided that there was no legal objection to such a procedure.) It is therefore possible to be taken for a woman or for a man and to live as a woman or as a man.

But when one's body is manipulated in the ways I have just described it has not been changed into that of a man or of a woman – it has become an intersex body. That is an issue that transsexuals find too painful to be acknowledged readily. Some of them, however, do put their feelings into words: "What am I?", a male-to-female transsexual asked me. "I'm an ambiguous sort of being." Many of them attach enormous importance to their neo-sex organ: "It's proof that I'm telling the truth when I say that I'm a woman [or a man]. If anybody doesn't believe what I say about my identity, I can show them my genitals." Thus it is clear that (I am thinking of Romain Gary's very distressing short story "Le Faux" in his *Gloire à nos illustres pionniers* where it was simply a matter of a nose) something false, pseudo-, a sham becomes, for the individual concerned, proof of the veracity of what he or she is saying: it is presented as a reality that takes on the quality of a symbol.

There must be some sense of doubt, of insecurity, of deep uncertainty working away inside for patients to take refuge in such claims; they are typical of the way the transsexual's mind works, and they could at least be considered psychotic statements.

Yet the patient feels happier, or at least less unhappy. Though not biologically male or female, there is an identification with masculine or feminine values prevalent in the culture in which he or she lives. There are rarely any regrets at having had the operation. (I shall come back to what becomes of patients who have undergone these operations.)

Of course, initially, those who discover the problem for the first time see the transsexual patient differently from the intersexed one: to be born without a penis evokes less intense feelings of dread than to have had one's penis removed. One feels sorry for the person who has had to adapt to the sad biological reality of not possessing a penis, but one recoils before the person who has taken the decision no longer to possess a penis. It is understandable for transsexuals to want some biological reason for their distress to be discovered, so that they may be seen as intersexed. They would then no longer have to run the risk of being considered mad: "It's my body, not my mind; I don't need to see a psychiatrist".

Some doctors think that such a serious disorder must, in the end, be of biological origin. Research has been done in order to show that the brain of the male-to-female transsexual is feminized while that of the female-to-male transsexual is masculinized, so that in fact both are to some extent intersexed. Between a legitimate working hypothesis and an act of faith that brooks no discussion, there is often very little room for manoeuvre. Studies that claim to have brought new evidence to light are often fraught with problems and their conclusions are at best debatable (that said, there is of course a need for more research).

Some physicians base their point of view on animal research experiments, often with rats, sometimes with monkeys. Some areas at the base of the brain are dimorphic, different in males and in females. Their function in rats, for example, is now known – they have to do with reproduction: lordosis (increased curvature of the lumbar region in the female when mounted by the male) in females, mounting behaviour in males. In Amsterdam, Zhou and his collaborators [1995], in a post-mortem study of the brains of six male-to-female transsexuals, found that the central subdivision of the bed nucleus of the stria terminalis was either similar in volume or slightly smaller than that of women (and therefore much smaller than that normally found in men). This brain area measures ± 2 mm^3. It took them eleven years to collect their sample of six cases. The main point is that no-one knows exactly what role the central subdivision of the bed nucleus of the stria terminalis plays in human beings, nor what its development should be. The authors of the report themselves acknowledge that there is no animal model of gender identity. They claim, nevertheless, that these results are compatible with possible brain impregnation *in utero* by hormones of the opposite sex.

This impregnation does play a part in congenital adrenal hyperplasia, a syndrome that leads to modifications in the external genitalia, tomboy behaviour in girls and perhaps a higher rate of homosexuality; there is, however, no refusal of their gender identity as female.

Other studies [Goy *et al.* 1988] have evidenced some behavioural masculinization (not all behaviour is affected) in female rhesus macaques after prenatal androgen impregnation; if this occurs early in gestation, there is in addition genital masculinization – which does not appear if the impregnation occurs later. None of the females was transformed into a behavioural male. As far as gender identity is concerned, how are we to know if these monkeys feel themselves to be male or female?

Attempts have also been made to study a whole series of biological markers that testify to changes in functional cerebral asymmetry in transsexuals and in homosexuals; these would indicate the presence *in utero* of hormonal effects. Such a perspective has to do with quantitative differences, with some overlapping of statistical distribution as between the sexes, and not with qualitative differences.

For example, hand preference has been investigated. Some studies show more left-handedness in transsexuals than in the control group (the difference, however, is slight). According to Geschwind and Galaburda [1987], left-handedness is associated with high levels of male hormones which slow down the development of the dominant left hemisphere, hence the dominance of the right hemisphere; in boys this gives rise both to language-based learning difficulties and to left-handedness. Not all researchers, however, would concur in the conclusions that can be drawn from such studies as regards transsexuals (or homosexuals, for that matter).

Sibling sex ratio has also been studied, as has birth order. As compared to control groups, boys who present gender identity disorder have more brothers than sisters; homosexuals have more brothers than heterosexuals have and more older brothers. Attempts have been made to link such factors to the mother's increased immune response to the Y-chromosome.

These studies on left-handedness, sex ratio, and birth order are an attempt to discover a purely biological explanation. They ignore the fact that the motor functions of left-handed people are not particularly well adapted to a world designed mainly for right-handed persons; the constraints they experience are more or less reinforced by social beliefs (in French, for example, there is a connection between *"gauche"*: clumsy, and *"gaucher"* = left-handed; this echoes the Latin word for left: *sinister*, etc.). Also, in the genesis of homosexuality, the relationships between brothers are not taken into account in these studies.

Fingerprints, which are formed between the thirteenth and nineteenth weeks of gestation, have been studied: females generally have fewer crests on the left hand than males do. The relative lengths of index and ring-finger have also been examined: in males the index finger is usually shorter than the ring-finger.

Cognitive studies highlight differences in performance in verbal tests (higher performances in females) and on spatial ones (in which males do better).

No study has been able to show whether or not these various "markers" are present simultaneously or are dissociated in transsexual people, in whom they would run contrary to the assigned identity. Though these markers have no direct connection with gender identity, they are said to involve possible hormonal effects *in utero*; it is these which could play a part in determining gender identity (constituting a brain that functions in the opposite way from the sex of the body).

With my colleagues I have treated several young children who rejected their assigned sex. The part played by the interactions between these children and their parents could not escape my notice. It is possible to modify an attitude of rejection concerning the assigned sex by promoting change in both parents and child. Transsexualism may arise from certain kinds of interaction between young children and their parents, whether or not there is some biological facilitation. Why should a person be held responsible for some disorder or other if it is the consequence of psychological events which occurred in infancy and childhood, but thought of as innocent if the disorder is the result of something biological that took place *in utero*? Why should he or she be considered mad in the former case and unfortunate in the latter?

A boy born without a penis demands to be treated as a man; we might feel this to be a distressing situation, and call in question the fundamental role played by the penis in the establishing of one's identity. But a transsexual who has his penis cut off (who fulfils Freud's fantasy according to which women are castrated men) and a transsexual who claims to be a man thanks to phalloplasty raise questions and cause anxiety in those who encounter such situations for the first time.

In my approach to the study of transsexualism, I shall try to put aside any *a priori* ideas and attempt to understand what these patients are going through.

Chapter Three

The psychoanalyst and the transsexual

Each transsexual is different from all others, even though their request for hormonal and surgical sex reassignment may be the same (or almost the same). This is a point that must never be forgotten, even if writing a short book on the subject means that we cannot enter into every detail. It is possible to search for and discover common factors in the way in which their minds work. But we have to pay close attention to the details of what transsexuals tell us; this may throw light on the particular path they have followed in life and perhaps even allow access to deeper levels of communication with them.

In the following paragraphs, I shall discuss first of all the case in which a transsexual consults, already convinced of the diagnosis and the consequent need for hormonal and surgical sex reassignment. The Resolution of the European Parliament voted on 12 September 1989 mentions the "psychiatric/psychotherapeutic differential diagnosis of transsexualism, by way of help with self-diagnosis". Though some patients *are* uncertain and ask for help in order to have a better grasp of what may be involved, many have already decided on their self-diagnosis – so that to talk of "help with self-diagnosis" is in fact a euphemism.

When a transsexual meets a psychoanalyst (or a psychotherapist), the latter expects that the person who is there in the same room will take his or her place on the mental stage and talk about conflicts, desires, past history, fantasies. With transsexuals, this is far from being the case. In their view there is no conflict underlying their request. It is not a question of a "desire" to belong to the opposite sex, but of the evidence that supports the claim that they *already belong* to the opposite sex. Their past history can be summarized in a few words – in fact most of the time they say that they remember nothing, or almost nothing, about their childhood. It is very rare for transsexuals to talk about their "fantasies". The psychoanalyst feels powerless, awkward in his or her willingness to understand, and stupid with comments (not interpretations – we are a far cry from that kind of intervention) which belong to another universe of discourse than that of the transsexual.

I. "That's just psycho-babble!"

The first and absolutely basic blunder to make is the following. (I shall take the example of Grace, an adolescent who consulted me unwillingly after a surgeon had refused to remove her breasts.) I said to her: "You would like to be a man." Her reply: "You don't understand a thing!" I corrected myself: "You mean that you are a man."

Yes, that was right: she was indeed a man, but she looked at me with such an air of condescension and pity at my stupidity ... It was worse than she had expected from a psychoanalyst. What could I do to resolve the difficulty in which I found myself? When I looked at her, I felt her to be a woman. Her voice was that of a woman; her wide hips were those of a woman, even though she was wearing a bomber jacket and thick shoes.

Ever since childhood she had done everything in her power to make other people acknowledge her identity as a boy. In fact she lived two lives: in school she was a girl; in her leisure activities she was a boy who played only with other boys under an assumed identity. But it all unravelled at puberty when her breasts betrayed her.

When she was a child she had been referred to a psychotherapist because of her violence. But she told her therapist nothing about her identity problem. If he were to have had any credibility in her eyes, he would have had to guess what it was all about: he did not guess anything at all; she never mentioned it; nothing happened.

One day I pointed out to her that the masculine first name she had chosen was the one which her mother had intended to give her if she had been a boy instead of a baby girl. "That's just psycho-babble!" It was really quite elementary ... but Grace missed several consecutive sessions after this discussion.

One of the very few comments she did accept was when I pointed out to her how much she was defending herself against the risk of letting herself experience any tender feelings: being a man means being tough.

When we stopped, her determination to have the operation had not changed at all. I do not know what help I may have been to her – perhaps none at all. But she taught me a great deal about how difficult it is to communicate with transsexuals when we cannot share their firm belief that they belong to the opposite sex. We do not want to hurt them, but we cannot (we must not) immediately abandon all attempt at understanding what is going on. The patient will choose whether or not to have the operation. I would never reject a patient who decides obstinately to follow the transsexual path he or she is on – but I am not a prescriber of surgical operations. I want to explore with the patient who or what he or she is and leave as many doors open as possible.

II. "I 'am', I don't 'want to be'"

How are we to understand a statement such as "I am a man", or "I am a woman"? Children who reject their assigned sex use such expressions only very rarely; what they do say is: "I would have liked to have been, to have been born ... When I grow up, I'll become ..." They pray to God every night that the metamorphosis will indeed occur. Despair takes hold of them at puberty when God fails to listen to them and the message from their body confirms the reality which they reject, which they hate, which they find unacceptable. It is then, as adolescents or adults, that they no longer say "I would like ...", but "I am ...", except for some patients who still ask themselves questions.

International classifications such as the ICD–10 (International Classification of Diseases, 10th edition, published under the aegis of the World Health Organization) or the DSM–IV (Diagnostic and Statistical Manual, 4th edition, published under the aegis of the American Psychiatric Association) give a toned-down version of what patients say in order to establish criteria that have to be met if they are to be designated transsexual.

In the International Classification of Diseases (ICD–10), category F64.0, *Transsexualism* is defined as:

> A desire to live and be accepted as a member of the opposite sex, usually accompanied by a sense of discomfort with, or inappropriateness of, one's anatomic sex, and a wish to have surgery and hormonal treatment to make one's body as congruent as possible with one's preferred sex.

Diagnostic directives: The transsexual identity has been present persistently for at least two years.

The disorder is not a symptom of another mental disorder such as schizophrenia nor associated with any other genetic or chromosomal sexual abnormality.

The Diagnostic and Statistical Manual of Mental Disorders (IV): Gender Identity Disorder of Childhood (302.6), Adolescence, or Adulthood (302.85), states that all of the following criteria must be met for the diagnosis of gender identity disorder to be made:

1. A strong desire or persistent cross-gender identification (not merely a desire for any perceived cultural advantages of being the other sex).
2. Persistent discomfort with his or her sex or sense of inappropriateness in the gender role of that sex.
3. The disturbance is not concurrent with a physical intersex condition.
4. The disturbance causes clinically significant distress or impairment in social, occupational or other areas of functioning.

Those remarks do not really describe what we hear when we listen attentively to such patients. They go far beyond "a sense of discomfort with, or inappropriateness of, one's anatomic sex", or a "persistent discomfort with his or her sex or sense of inappropriateness in the gender role of that sex". It is not a matter of "discomfort"; it is a refusal, a complete rejection of their assigned sex; their anatomic sex is completely unacceptable to them and horrifies them. Children make the astonishing discovery that he/she is not the girl/boy they thought they were – they wanted to be – and manifest by all the means at their disposal that they cannot accept their assigned sex. Gradually, their position hardens; they no longer feel what they experience to be a desire but a simple matter of fact. Transsexuals are said to have the *unshakeable conviction* of belonging to the opposite sex. We could enter into interminable discussions about shades of meaning between "belief" and "conviction". But transsexuals need to maintain their conviction and to convince other people; other people have a major part to play in acknowledging the sex to which we belong. Transsexuals seem to possess a fanatical desire to obtain what they demand, even if it means putting their life at risk. The ICD–10 mentions "a wish to have surgery and hormonal treatment". We could of course use the term *wish* when referring to transsexuals, but we must not forget the sheer strength with which transsexuals fight to obtain this treatment.

The expressions used by transsexuals are much more incisive. They convey the feeling that they cannot live within their assigned identity. It is not simply the fact that their request for hormonal and surgical sex reassignment has been present for at least two years; it is because they are experiencing a problem situation that goes to the very heart of their being. That implies the expression of something either inscribed in their body (in their brain) or established during the first few years of life. At any rate transsexuals have always felt that they do not exist otherwise than as members of the opposite sex. As regards the assigned sex, the transsexual feels like "a stranger in [his or her] body", as Domenico Di Ceglie and David Freedman put it [1998]; they talk of their body as if it were a foreign envelope floating around them, inside which lurks their "true self". When we try to put a label on this syndrome, we find ourselves in serious difficulty: the whole problem situation is focused on being. It is not a psychosis, nor a neurosis, nor a perversion, nor a psychosomatic disorder – it could be linked to *anorexia nervosa* in adolescence. It stands at the crossroads, at the outer frontier of all these possibilities. We could say borderline state, perhaps, narcissistic pathology, encapsulated delusion – but even then the very nature of transsexualism, irreducible to anything else, escapes us.

III. "I wonder . . ."

The presentation that I have just made concerns the kind of transsexual that my colleagues who make use of the distinction would call "true" or "primary". In these patients, what I call the "identity component" is the dominant element.

However, patients who come for hormonal and surgical sex reassignment have not all followed such a clear-cut, linear path in life. Some patients still have doubts about what they are and ask to be helped to answer that question. They are terribly afraid of being thought mad if ever they dare to talk about their experience of life. A psychoanalyst may perhaps not divert them away from the transsexual path, but at least the advantage is that they will be able to talk to somebody about their experience without being rejected.

Lost in agonizing uncertainty, they give the impression of being psychotic, schizophrenic: a state that gradually fades as they dare more and more to assert themselves as members of the opposite sex.

It is by giving this kind of impression that a certain number of children have "incubated" their transsexualism. Their family never noticed that they were rejecting their assigned sex. There are more boys than girls who do this, and they tend to be isolated, withdrawn and often low-achievers in school. During adolescence they see or read or hear something in the media that mentions transsexualism, and then it all clicks together: they realize at last what their suffering is all about; and they feel better, because henceforth they have a goal in life – to succeed in obtaining appropriate surgery.

As far as girls are concerned, besides those who behave as tomboys, there are others, apparently feminine, who have pondered over the idea that they were really boys because, from about age six or seven years, they have felt attracted only to girls. They say to themselves – nobody says this to them, they say it to themselves – "It's homosexuality. And homosexuality isn't normal. But I'm normal. So, if I feel attracted to girls, I must be a boy." It is only much later that they give themselves any kind of masculine appearance.

To the observer, in cases of female-to-male transsexualism, there is a "homosexual component". But for the persons concerned there is nothing homosexual about it. Besides, their sexual activity is not like that of women who declare themselves to be homosexual; there is no reciprocity in their amorous exchanges. Female-to-male transsexuals caress their partner, but do not allow themselves to be caressed (there are a few exceptions to this general rule). The partner's pleasure is important, but their own does not appear to matter; they are perhaps afraid of it. In that relationship, the female-to-male transsexual wants to be treated as a man, and this is indeed what occurs.

In men, almost exclusively (Stoller mentions only three cases of female transvestites; women do not usually experience much erotic pleasure in dressing up as men), there is also a "transvestite component". In the most exemplary of cases, transvestism is quite different from transsexualism, even though for quite some time the same word was used to describe both groups in English (transvestites) and in German (*Transvestiten*). In French some translators have hesitated to use the word *transvestis*; it is, however, necessary to use the term in order to avoid any confusion with the simple fact of wearing clothes more suitable to the opposite sex (cross-dressing, *travestissement* in French). Transvestism is a specific syndrome in which the individual experiences the compulsive need and orgasmic pleasure in dressing up as a woman, in looking at himself in the mirror dressed in women's clothes (perhaps photographing himself), and in imagining himself to be a woman, masturbating as he does so. The transvestite sets great store by his penis; he makes use of it just as much to masturbate as to have coitus. But in his sexual relationship with a woman (he is often a married man), his ecstatic pleasure comes from imagining himself to be a woman. His childhood was that of a little boy, though there would have been some cross-dressing phases, usually towards the end of the latency period. Stoller thinks that the boy must have been dressed up as a woman against his wishes and then laughed at, his manliness being belittled in the process; his transvestism in adulthood would thus be an intentional and proactive away of turning the tables on such a humiliation, transforming it into a triumph.

It can happen, however, that quite late on in life it is not enough for the transvestite to imagine himself as a woman; he declares that he wants to become one. This situation is called secondary trans-sexualism, as in the case where a man who has hitherto lived his life as a homosexual decides to become a woman, often with the idea of living officially with his male partner.

In dealing with transvestites, the psychoanalyst has a quite different experience from that with transsexuals *stricto sensu*. There is a "pleas-ure bonus" in the way they behave; they are not prepared to give up their pleasure, whereas transsexuals are overwhelmed by the suffering of their existential drama. Some talk of perversion in referring to trans-vestites; that term has connotations of rejection and I have never liked it. When one can see in the pervert who feels the need to hurt his or her partner a child who has been abused or humiliated in some way and is seeking revenge, as Stoller describes the situation, it becomes easier to control one's negative counter-transference. But is it possible to cure such a person? The most we can do is to invite the pervert to associate freely to each of the details in those scenarios and scripts, to re-live the childhood experiences that are being repeated in his or her adult behaviour, to try to discover what it might mean, to understand him- or herself better, and perhaps to live with greater equanimity afterwards. [See the treatment of Mrs G. in Stoller (1974).]

Sometimes transvestites will make do with the administration of hormones and go no further; hormones do have a spectacular effect in that they suppress the erections that created so much anxiety in the patient. In consultation once I saw a patient who became extremely aggressive when he realized that he would not immediately obtain what he was demanding. It was difficult to believe in his irrepressible identity as a woman because he had a beard and a man's haircut – though he had travelled all the way by train dressed as a woman ...

When I asked him why he wore his hair cut short, he replied that his employer would not agree to his having long hair. Why did he have a beard? He replied that his wife felt that when he was beardless he looked too much like his sister, whom she detested. He was apparently impervious to the incongruity of his appearance. I dreaded meeting him a second time – but he was as gentle as a lamb when he came in; another doctor had prescribed hormones, which calmed him down wonderfully and that was all he was looking for.

IV. "I like it"

In two rulings in December 1992, the Cour de Cassation [the French final appellate court], bowing to the pressure of a judgement of the European Court of Human Rights, agreed to allow change of sex in the civil status records on condition that the "syndrome of transsexualism" be averred and that the transformation had been practised as a therapeutic measure. The court was wary of situations in which certain people would attempt to be changed into women for "professional" reasons – as music-hall artistes, for example, or in order to be more satisfying as prostitutes.

As I mentioned in Chapter I, the first reported case of the successful transformation of a man into a woman was that of George, later Christine, Jorgenson. George had been a GI, and was a photographer by trade; Christine was a music-hall artiste and wrote her autobiography. Others have become artistes, such as Coccinelle in France, who also published her story in a book. In Thailand there are lots of alluring dancing-girls ... A female Israeli singer won a European song contest. Those men became not only women, but beautiful women at that – something that was very important to them.

Young men – some minors, some adult – who, dressed as women, work as prostitutes in the Bois de Boulogne have been referred to me for consultation. I find myself plunged into a milieu with which I am not particularly familiar. I listen to them talking of the misery of their life, in the cold of winter and the darkness of the night, and of the assaults to which they fall victim. However, although they may want to change their sex, they do not want to change their ... profession. It takes my breath away to hear them say: "I like it. I like being attractive and charming. I would like to be the most beautiful woman in the world." One of them managed to make his breasts grow, thanks to hormones he had procured illegally, in order to please his boyfriend; then, when the latter abandoned him, he had them cut off. But now he wants them back, because he has a new boyfriend who would like him to have breasts.

These young people are referred to me in the hope that I might be able to help them. But they already have a long history of erratic family life; they combine extreme poverty in material terms with the lack of any emotional support. They cannot be expected to turn up regularly and on time for their appointments – they appear and disappear. There is a need for other care facilities which could provide long-term support. They are seized upon by institutions that are useful in that they draw the attention of these young men to protecting themselves against the AIDS virus, but which, at the same time, encourage them in their ideas about changing sex. This has little to do with primary trans-sexualism – yet at the same time, they could hardly be said not to have problems of gender identity. In addition their whole personality has lost its structure and they are de-socialized to such a degree that they are far beyond anything a psychoanalyst might do.

There are also people who say that they take up prostitution as a temporary measure, in order to earn enough money for the necessary surgery (though, in France, the operation is paid for by the social security system) and to set themselves up in life. And I do know of some – very few – who have succeeded in this. The others go on prostituting themselves after the operation. In fact some begin a career in prostitution after the operation. Prostitution involves only male-to-female transsexuals; but I have heard of one case of a female-to-male transsexual who became a pimp after the sex-change operation.

Chapter Four

Treatment

E ven though we may think that "sex change" is a mad response to a mad request, it does exist, and it is legal or even commonplace in some countries (although it does remain banned in others). Patients who really want such treatment will manage to find it. And, as Stoller writes [1968: 247]:

> The general rule that applies to the treatment of the transsexual is that no matter what one does – including nothing – it will be wrong.

We are faced with a problem which defeats us; there is no correct solution.

I. Hormonal and surgical sex reassignment

Doctors are unquestionably in good faith when they think that, after a sex change, patients suffer less; they say that a new life is dawning for these patients even though they do not feel euphoria, even though there are still difficulties, and even though they will gradually have to realize that the media have been less than truthful – they are not wholly men or women in the same way as those born men or women are: they do nevertheless feel better and happier.

Those doctors endeavour to establish criteria for recommending hormonal and surgical sex reassignment: they have to make sure that the patient will be able to withstand the operation and derive some benefit from it. It is a mutilation (the ablation of healthy organs) and as such legal action could be taken against the doctors involved if they fail to have their intervention acknowledged as therapeutic (via a declaration to the board of the relevant medical association);

in France, the cost of the operation is met by the social security system. It is a remarkable fact that showing videotapes of these operations to prospective patients in no way discourages them, although any ordinary person would find it difficult to go on watching.

Prescribing doctors set great store by the distinction between primary and secondary transsexualism. Clinical experience, however, shows that these issues are much more complex, and when we do have the opportunity of seeing cases which they consider to be primary we are sometimes far from agreeing with that opinion."Primary trans-sexualism" would seem to mean that ever since early childhood such patients have felt that they belong to the opposite sex and have con-stantly manifested this without hesitation and without making any concession to their assigned sex. Having completed their military service, married, had children – these are no minor concessions to one's assigned sex which coincides with all the main aspects of the bio-logical sex (except, perhaps, with the "sex of the brain", which is *de facto* invisible). Patients, however, tend to argue that they have done all that in order to "normalize" their situation. It does mean, of course, that the biological possibilities of their assigned sex have remained intact, whereas no possibility of having intercourse or procreating as members of the opposite sex exists.

The criteria for diagnosis have now been more or less systematized. The Resolution of the European Parliament dated 12 September 1989 talks of "self-diagnosis"; the role of physicians would thus seem to be limited to helping patients to make their own diagnosis and to confirming this. The Harry Benjamin International Gender Dysphoria Association has drawn up a set of minimum guidelines which are revised periodically. Some doctors follow these guidelines; others adopt their own procedures [see, for example, Chiland and Cordier 2000]. It is generally agreed that there must be a minimum of two years' observation with a real-life test, during which the patient lives as a member of the opposite sex and tries out the hormone treatment (it sometimes happens that there is a hiatus between what the patient imagines and what he or she really feels once confronted with the initial stages of the transformation). In France, the decision is taken, not by a single doctor, but by a panel composed of a psychiatrist, a surgeon and an endocrinologist. In following that procedure the prescribing doctors rarely take into account any children born before the transsexual father or mother decides on a change of sex; Bernard Cordier and Thierry Gallarda [Cordier, Chiland and Gallarda 2001], however, do not prescribe transformation in the case of a parent of a child who is still a minor. The problem is not that there could be a consequential disturbance of the latter's gender identity or sexual preference; it is the resultant situation as a whole which might prove stressful for the child.

Some patients are (im)patient, and cannot bear any postponement in carrying out the surgical procedure. They go abroad and consult physicians whose guidelines are much more flexible and who agree to operate much more readily. I have met patients who have been through such operations with no ill-effects – but I have met others who are surgical catastrophes (with necrosis of the pubis, for example) or psychiatric disasters (one patient, for example, became psychotic, tried to commit suicide on several occasions and, finally, wanted his original male sex to be restored to him).

There is a rumour in the transsexual community that, aesthetically speaking, the results of the operation are better in countries other than France – hence the idea that they have to save up considerable sums of money in order to have the operation.

Those who practise the operation sometimes make a commercial enterprise out of it, a fact that Stoller found regrettable. He wanted hormonal and surgical sex reassignment to remain experimental and to be practised in a research setting, and as the years went by he became more and more restrictive with respect to the operation. Sometimes surgeons have the demiurge feeling that they are creating a new human being. Others, however, do ask themselves questions about what they are doing. In France, until now, surgeons have carried out these operations in the public sector, without any financial profit and without devoting themselves wholly to this one activity (in some foreign countries, there are surgeons who do nothing other than cut off penises or do phalloplasty). Unfortunately, sufficient attention has not been given over to research. This could have included follow-up studies of patients over many years in order to evaluate properly the long-term results of hormonal and surgical sex reassignment. In France doctors are reluctant to do so, believing that patients should be free to disappear into anonymity and to build a new life for themselves. Indeed, among the initial three doctors who take the decision, the one whom patients consult regularly without any constraint other than therapeutic necessity is the endocrinologist, for a theoretically annual check-up. Regular monitoring of this kind is necessary, because patients have to take opposite-sex hormones for the rest of their life.

As far as surgery itself is concerned, complications may set in: stenosis of the neo-vagina, fistulae, urinary-tract complications, penile gangrene after phalloplasty, etc. These often go unmentioned or their importance is played down. It is true, of course, that attempts are being made to improve surgical techniques, but these are, all the same, procedures that are by no means innocuous.

The person who used to live normally without medical attention henceforth has to be kept under long-term medical observation.

II. Integration in real life

It would be a highly significant step were we able to evaluate the results of hormonal and surgical sex reassignment in order to continue this kind of palliative treatment, in the absence of any curative measure. Long-term follow-up studies all leave much to be desired [for more details on outcome research, see Chiland 1997].

Not all patients who have had an operation are seen afterwards, even when the operation took place in a teaching or public-sector hospital where research is regularly carried out. Often the sample population in such studies is small and restricted to one sex; yet there are significant differences as between the sexes.

The lapse of time between operation and assessment is variable, but often short. It is only in the long term that certain disastrous consequences appear, such as in the case of Agnes which I shall discuss infra, or Ruth Shumaker, as reported by Stephen B. Levine [1983, 1984] (Ruth committed suicide one year after publishing an article on the magnificent outcome of her hormonal and surgical sex reassignment.)

Attempts have been made to use suicide as an argument against hormonal and surgical sex reassignment, but suicide is a rare occurrence, perhaps no more and no less frequent a phenomenon than that occurring before the sex reassignment procedure. Threats of suicide are put forward in order to obtain reassignment and can make quite an impression on some doctors; others have pointed out, however, that such threats are more often than not indicative of a negative outcome of the reassignment procedure.

There is little regret when the decision to operate is taken after a period of careful observation. There may be some upset at the results of the surgery rather than as regards the operation itself. (Although it is said that the results of surgery are poor in France, only one patient out of 49 whom I have seen in consultation at variable intervals of time after the operation complained about the outcome.)

It should be noted too that even if the patient asks for psychotherapeutic help after the operation (and this is happening with increasing frequency), he or she still maintains that it would not have been possible to do without the sex change.

Were we to be meticulous, a control group would be required. But this is impossible to set up – we cannot "randomize" or draw lots to decide who will have the treatment and who will not; anyway, those who are refused the operation will simply go elsewhere to have it done. There have been attempts to compare patients who have had an operation with those who have not, but these are not equivalent groups.

The less "primary" the transsexualism, the less satisfying the results.

In contrast to the patient's overall satisfaction, social integration remains a problem for those for whom this was already the case before their operation; here there is a clear difference between male-to-female transsexuals and their female-to-male counterparts. Male-to-female transsexuals appear to form two sub-groups, one of which is similar to female-to-male transsexuals, the other presenting associated pathological states (co-morbidity).

Before their change in civil status, some patients, especially male-to-female transsexuals, do not to manage to stay in regular employment. They emphasize the problems that their identity documents create for them, since these papers (social security card, identity card) no longer reflect their actual appearance, as well as the everyday difficulties which they encounter (credit card, passport).

Some patients, usually female-to-male transsexuals, find more or less legal solutions to such problems. They may quite officially manage to obtain a different social security number (which begins, according to the French National Institute of Statistics and Economic Studies nomenclature, always with "1" for men and "2" for women – thereby immediately revealing a person's sex; this would be the case even though the first name could apply to either sex or the person's identity card has been tampered with); or they succeed in convincing their employer to accept them and their problem. Sometimes, as high academic achievers, they hold positions of responsibility; even graduates of the Ecole Polytechnique (the prestigious engineering college in Paris specializing in science and technology, with a competitive entrance examination) may be transsexual. Others have a background of repeated low achievement in their academic life and practically no professional training; they live on various kinds of social security benefit (minimum social income, allowance for handicapped adults, unemployment benefit, disability pension, etc.); the vast majority of these cases are male-to-female transsexuals.

After the operation and modification to civil status records, professional integration remains something of a problem for a number of transsexuals, as several follow-up studies have shown. In my own personal sample, 9 male-to-female transsexuals out of 22 (41%) live on social security benefits, while only 1 out of 27 female-to-male transsexuals (4%) is temporarily out of work; all the others are in employment.

Social integration varies from person to person. Many complain of loneliness. They find it hard to talk truthfully about themselves and their background, and this makes it difficult for them to have close friendships. As far as partners are concerned transsexuals are unsure of what to tell them and when: male-to-female transsexuals sometimes try to hide the fact that they have changed sex; female-to-male transsexuals, who have visible scars and a particular kind of "penis", cannot avoid saying something – occasionally, they say that they are intersexed. The manner in which they succeed in integrating their experience plays a decisive role. Of the transsexuals whom I have met and who seem to me to be well integrated, the happiest are female-to-male transsexuals; the defining moment for them was when they found a woman partner (who up until then had had exclusively heterosexual intercourse) who loves them as a man, they are in a stable partner relationship, and, in addition, they have parents who accept them, as well as a wide circle of friends.

In the best of cases transsexuals who have had the requisite surgery talk of re-birth, of liberation, of how at last they feel themselves to be who they really are.

If they intended to live as members of the opposite sex, they have reached their goal. If their aim was to be men or women in the fullest sense of these terms, they cannot but be disenchanted or even terribly disappointed.

III. Plausibility

One of the factors which facilitates social integration is the plausibility of the person as regards his or her target sex.

In the case of male-to-female transsexuals, it is possible, while walking in the street, to encounter women who are indistinguishable from all other women; they feel that they "make the grade" and indeed they do, completely. Some have the appearance of starlets or pin-up girls; others retain something of their former masculinity, which therefore betrays them and leaves them open to persecution in public transport – "drag queen" name-calling. A higher proportion than in the general population (as Benjamin had already pointed out) have always been more or less beardless, but some are distressed by the facial hair showing through their make-up even when this is quite thickly laid on; hormone treatment does not make their beard disappear, so that they are obliged to have recourse to hair removal procedures (electrical or laser) which sometimes leave marks. Those who are tall, with large hands and feet, retain their masculine build. In many, their voice is and will stay low-pitched. "When I phone for a job interview, I am immediately ruled out – I say 'I'm Ms ...' and the person at the other end of the line hears a masculine voice ..." Sometimes an operation on the vocal chords is suggested, along with speech therapy. Their Adam's apple is more or less prominent at first, and there have been attempts to shave the cartilage (tracheal shave). Deportment lessons have also been proposed: leaving anatomy aside, it is obvious that they are not spontaneously "feminine". Some clinics abroad offer all these services as adjuncts to surgery.

These details only go to show that, even if the hypothesis concerning areas at the base of the brain developing in the female direction were to be confirmed, the rest of the body does not keep pace with this. "I am a woman," says the person concerned, but this "naturalness" is obtained only by artificial means. Some in fact demand a whole series of different cosmetic surgery operations, and find surgeons willing to carry these out. Is there such a thing as a "masculine nose" or a "feminine" one? How many of us are men with their mother's nose or women with their father's without necessarily feeling any ambiguity? This situation comes close to dysmorphophobia, in which the patient can never be satisfied with his or her physical appearance.

Female-to-male transsexuals are often quite short, with small hands and feet; their voice breaks, however, and their beard grows thanks to the hormone treatment. We may quite easily feel that we are in the presence of a man. Stoller has written about his first encounter with a transsexual. His friends [Worden and Marsh] were done with their project (the first serious piece of research ever done on transsexualism), but still had an appointment with a patient whom they had never met but who could be categorized as a "transsexual woman" (a biological female who nonetheless considered herself to be a man):

They asked me to see her to tell her the research was finished. Shortly before the appointment hour, I was approaching stupor at a committee meeting in a conference room with a glass wall that allowed us to see people pass. A man walked by; I scarcely noticed him. A moment later, a secretary announced my eleven o'clock patient. And to my astonishment, the patient was not what I expected – a woman who acted masculine and in the process was a bit too much, grimly and pathetically discarding her femininity. Instead it was a man, unremarkable, natural appearing (years before, he had had a mastectomy and a panhysterectomy, and he had been taking hormones) – an ordinary man (and eight years' follow-up until his death never changed that impression). [Stoller 1985: 4]

A higher number of female-to-male transsexuals than in the general population have a moustache or a beard: "Anybody addressing me as 'Mrs' or 'Miss' would look ridiculous."

In fact, our initial decision as to whether the person in front of us is a man or a woman is based on surface criteria. What goes on in the mind is much more difficult to grasp.

IV. "Changing what people have in their minds"

Faced with the realization that medical science is unable to change completely a man into a woman or a woman into a man, some patients have said to me: "Doctors will have to become able to change what people have in their minds."

Obviously it would be a more satisfying kind of treatment with no need for mutilation or for transforming a healthy organism into an unhealthy one. Patients would not have to cope with this break in their history which causes them so much difficulty socially and professionally. One can only hope that such a treatment will one day become a possibility.

When the first reports of cases of hormonal and surgical sex reassignment were published, some psychoanalysts argued that this "treatment" was absurd and that transsexuals ought to be psychoanalysed. They believed that this syndrome was an ordinary form of neurosis. The problem was that these patients very rarely consulted a psychoanalyst, and if they did so, the psychoanalyst was powerless to set the situation to rights. One famous example is that of Renée Richards, an ophthalmologist and tennis champion, who has published her autobiography [Richards 1983]. Stoller claims never to have psychoanalysed a transsexual (he is referring to true transsexuals, those I have called "transsexuals *à la* Stoller"); when he suggested psychoanalysis, for example to a male-to-female transsexual known as Agnes, he-changed-into-she refused, in spite of the distress she found herself in.

Nowadays some transsexuals who have had the requisite operation do request psychotherapy or even psychoanalysis – sometimes several years after the operation – and are indeed capable of deriving some benefit from it. They still maintain, all the same, that they could not have done without the operation itself.

Appropriate psychological treatment still remains to be invented. A psychoanalyst or psychotherapist may however be able to help transsexuals.

In one report, some adolescents or young men in whom the homosexual component was dominant gave up the idea of having the operation and decided to acknowledge their homosexuality [Sesé-Léger 1997]. Other patients, while resolutely maintaining their wish to have hormonal and surgical treatment, have derived some benefit from psychotherapy, in particular as regards their ability to communicate and to engage in relationships. Others have found support for coping with the difficulties that the "transformation" brings in its wake. They found it very helpful to have somewhere where they could talk about their situation in all its reality, since the prescribing physician does not always have sufficient time to spend with them.

Childhood is one of the most favourable periods for psychotherapy. Some of those who specialize in hormonal and surgical sex reassignment, such as Ira Pauly, acknowledge this. The situation is not yet decided: children's minds do not yet function in the way that the transsexual adult's does. Help should be offered not only to the child but also to both parents. As the parents gradually come to understand their contribution to their child's behaviour and their underlying attitudes towards masculinity and femininity, the child may begin to change. Will these changes be long-lasting? What becomes of children who have been treated in this way?

Richard Green's study, *The "Sissy Boy Syndrome" and the Development of Homosexuality* [Green 1987], failed to find any major difference between very feminine-like boys who had received treatment and those who had not. The treatment procedures themselves, however, were diverse to say the least and often not intensive. Fifteen years later, out of 44 boys who had been very feminine-like as children, three-quarters turned out to be homosexual or bisexual (only one was transsexual) and the remaining quarter were heterosexual. Therefore, not all children who present a gender identity disorder turn out to be transsexuals. Such research ought to be pursued; studies are being carried out at the Child and Adolescent Gender Identity Disorder Clinic in Toronto, under the direction of Kenneth Zucker, and at the Tavistock Clinic in London in a unit under the direction of Domenico Di Ceglie.

At adolescence young people are much less likely to abandon their rejection of their assigned sex. It is however still worth while to attempt a *trial psychotherapy* as recommended by Leslie Lothstein, who worked for several years in the Case Western Reserve University in Cleveland and who has considerable experience in this field.

Chapter Five

How the transsexual's mind works

One of the reasons that makes a psychotherapeutic approach with transsexuals so difficult has to do with the way their mind works. The type of functioning which I am about to describe is, to all intents and purposes, shared by all transsexuals in whom the identity component is a decisive factor.

I. On the defensive

"Transsexuals lie," one of my fellow doctors tells me. In fact, they say what they imagine will force the doctor to agree to the transformation which they so much want to have.

One young woman, pleasant and forthcoming, spoke to me in a way that made me feel sympathetic towards her. She told me that it all went back to her childhood: she had always refused to wear skirts or dresses. Later, I met her mother who showed me some of the very few photographs which had survived the *auto-da-fé* of the family album which the patient had instigated when she took the decision to live as a man, towards the end of her adolescence, after a love affair had broken up: I could see an adolescent girl of about 15, with a pony-tail, wearing a Liberty print dress that she had sewn herself.

Since that experience, I listen to what patients tell me and keep it in the back of my mind until it can be verified. Doctors who prescribe hormonal and surgical sex reassignment ask to meet the patient's family, look at childhood photographs etc. in order to confirm the diagnosis of primary transsexualism.

After the operation, patients are able to talk more freely. Whenever I have pointed this out to them, they reply: "Well, during the treatment, you never know what to say next, you're afraid to say something that could be interpreted in such-and-such a manner. You're on your guard. Now there's spontaneity, I have nothing more to win or to lose, I've at last obtained ... At last I am what I am." Others say: "I probably wouldn't have answered your questions if you'd asked me before the operation," or: "You're in a kind of perverse way of functioning, every word you say is based on what you imagine the person you're talking to is going to think; because whatever you say to a neuropsychiatrist – who, and you're well aware of the fact, will be partly responsible for taking you where you want to go – is going to be interpreted according to his or her reading and decoding of your words."

Sexuality especially gives rise to statements in which such patients deny any experience of masturbation or any sexual experience at all. Transsexuals exchange information: "You're told 'You mustn't demand anything to do with sexual matters because what these people want is for transsexualism not to be a sexual thing at all'." Contrary to what some of my colleagues would say, transsexuals do have sexual desires, but some of them have difficulty in putting up with these. Male-to-female transsexuals are distressed and anxious when they have an erection, because it reminds them of the hated penis that they want to see disappear. Female-to-male transsexuals cannot stand the excitement their drives produce in them: although they care very much about giving their partner pleasure, they do not really seek this for themselves (which is not the case with female homosexuals).

II. Everything on the body's stage, nothing on the mind's

Transsexuals do not come forward with any psychological problem or conflict. All that they suffer from is "an error of Nature". Nature made a mistake (not God, though many are believers, they do not think that it was God who wanted them to have the body they have). The plans were wrongly carried out; it is almost as though in the body-envelope shop, somebody hung on their soul an envelope intended for the opposite sex – that is the impression one gets when one hears them talk of how foreign their body feels to them.

They consult a psychiatrist only because they are obliged to do so if they want a green light for the operation. They do not think that they have any psychological problems. They want "restorative" surgery. Every honest surgeon will tell them that there are limits to what one can do in surgical transformation, but often patients do not properly take this in.

Once their complaint and their request expressed, they have nothing else to say. They protect themselves against engaging in a transference relationship. They feel that the person sitting opposite them wants to entrap them and make them abandon their project; they are ready to take to their heels.

It is true that doctors, including the prescribing physician, are not immediately unconditional allies as far as carrying out their project is concerned. Their duty is to assess whether a given patient fulfils the criteria for the procedure which the panel has adopted. A consultation for gender identity disorder ought not to be a mere programme for hormonal and surgical sex reassignment; there should be sufficient resources at hand for those who do not meet the criteria and whom we ought not to leave simply to deal alone with their distress.

Transsexuals do not lend themselves easily to any exploration of what goes on in their mind; they want to have things "done" as quickly as possible. It is only in the aftermath that these patients are sometimes prepared to acknowledge that the time taken was not entirely useless.

III. Infantile amnesia, splitting and denial

The psychiatrist's exploration concerns itself mainly with the patient's childhood. People seeking hormonal and surgical sex reassignment say that they have always felt themselves to be members of the opposite sex and have behaved as such. But, having said that, they very quickly answer: "I don't remember". What kind of infantile amnesia is this?

Some say: "I don't want to remember", which in itself throws some light on the issue. It seems that, by dint of not wanting to remember, patients manage to wipe out all memories of things they find too embarrassing – for example, the painful recall of facts incompatible with the identity they demand for themselves. Bisexuality is something transsexuals find intolerable; it appears only in the guise of "my body belongs to one sex, my soul to the opposite one", and then has to be got rid of. This is not repression, which would be unintentional and give rise to the return of the repressed; what has in fact taken place is a form of splitting. For a man, to remember that he once had periods is both bizarre and agonizing, just as it would be for a woman to remember that she once had erections. In transsexuals who undertake psychological treatment after their operation, what they can then say of their childhood becomes gradually much more detailed as they become able to acknowledge that, somewhere inside, they do have "parts" of the sex they reject, and begin to accept these.

I have only once met a patient who said to me: "Do you want me to tell you about my childhood fantasies?" Noticing the look of surprise on my face, he added: "I can speak your psychoanalytic language." His fantasies were rich in content and his past history different from that of most transsexuals.

Denial is expressed in statements such as those I have quoted in Chapter II: phalloplasty (a false penis, which is neither an original one nor functional) and the neo-vagina (which may be functional) are presented as proof of the veracity of their discourse: "I am a man/I am a woman". One patient to whom the surgeon said: "It's a simulation," replied: "No, Doctor, it's a symbol".

The denial lies perhaps in the fact of being convinced that one is a woman when one's whole body is male and one has to learn how to behave as a woman, or that one is a man when one's whole body is female and one has to make an effort to behave as a man. Where does this internal constraint come from? As I have shown, some would defend the hypothesis that it comes from the organization of the brain *in utero*; for others, the main factor is the early relationship between the child and his or her parents, together with the interpretations that the child makes of the parents' communications (Winnicott used to say that the child's illness belongs to the child [1965: 74]; children are not a kind of passive soft wax on which the outside world simply leaves its imprint).

What is undoubtedly denial is the belief that, thanks to hormones and surgery, one's body has changed, whereas in fact all that has occurred is the removal of the external signs of one sex and the imitating of the external signs of the opposite sex – *appearances* have changed. When transsexuals are reminded of this, the hurt they feel unfortunately becomes even more intense. Yet a therapist cannot but be the ambassador of reality: maintaining the illusion would mean going from illusion to delusion.

There are candidates for hormonal and surgical sex reassignment who could quite spontaneously pass for members of the opposite sex. Most manage this only by means of various devices and hormones. Actors who play transsexuals do so marvellously, without their being particularly concerned by the problem on a personal level: I can think of the boy in the film *Ma Vie en Rose* (*My Life in Pink*) by Alain Berliner or of the young woman in *Boys Don't Cry* by Kimberley Peirce. These actors are wonderful *impersonators*, as we say in English. Some little boys who reject their assigned sex are effeminate; others are very feminine as well as being good imitators, like Lance, Stoller's exemplary case. Natural, imitation, devices – again we come up against the question "what is 'masculine', what is 'feminine'?"

As the years go by, we see patients being transformed and, for some at least, becoming perfectly plausible. Yet, when they say: "I've always been a woman" (or a man), they are talking about their inner feelings; they have forgotten just how much it cost them to – apparently – become one.

Transvestites have more to say about their past life as boys and men. In school they were little boys. They may well have chosen very masculine professions, and completed their military service without drawing attention to themselves. They have married; sometimes they say that, in bed, they were not exactly the mightiest of warriors, though others have had passionate love affairs just like other men. They have had children. I am not saying that, in childhood, they did not suffer from gender identity disorder, especially with respect to the pleasure they took in dressing up as girls, usually secretly; but part of their identity was masculine. Can this disorder still be linked to the smaller volume of the central subdivision of the bed nucleus of the stria terminalis? I must admit that I have my doubts; yet colleagues who are convinced of the biological origin of gender identity disorders think that this is indeed the case. They explain the delay in asking for hormonal and surgical sex reassignment by the patient's attempts to "normalize" the situation by marrying and by trying to play the man's role – one that, in fact, is foreign to them. Their female state is not expressed through morphological changes in their genitalia, through an inability to have coitus and to procreate, or through a female habitus manifested as such from the outset; the irrepressible need they experience is for the accoutrements which have "feminine" connotations in the society in which they live: clothes, handbag, make-up, nail varnish. When we see these transvestites who have become secondary transsexuals – in what I call a belated vocation (they are usually between 40 and 70 years of age) – alternate between their feminine presentation and their masculine one, the feeling we have is that of something uncanny: we go to fetch our patient in the waiting-room, and fail to recognize him/her. Until then we had seen a dignified middle-class lady, admittedly heavily made-up and with a deep voice, and now there is a handsome man with a quite definitely receding hairline ... How can they believe in their feminine "identity"? What does this pressing need signify, the need for which they are ready to sacrifice their family life, their social life, their work? A few manage to stop themselves sliding all the way down the slope towards "transformation", but with considerable difficulty and great distress.

IV. Nosology on the spot

Attempts have been made to give this way of functioning a nosological label. Until now I have not succeeded in doing this to any satisfactory extent, even though I have tried out various ways of formulating it. It is true, of course, that I find it more important to establish contact with someone and to try to understand him or her than to look for an appropriate label.

One of the first to have studied transsexualism in France, Jean-Marc Alby – his work is relatively unknown because his medical thesis, entitled "A contribution to the study of trans-sexualism", has never been published (he sat his *viva* in 1956) – clearly realized that trans-sexualism stands at a crossroads, at the "frontier" of all kinds of pathology.

It would therefore be tempting to speak of a "borderline" state. I have on occasion yielded to that temptation without feeling satisfied. In the first place, the term does not have exactly the same meaning for different writers. For Otto Kernberg, borderline states are characterized by identity diffusion with conservation of reality-testing. The trans-sexual's identity disorder could be likened to an identity diffusion. And it is true that, in every domain that does not involve that identity, their sense of reality is intact.

In a paper written in 1999, André Green gives the following description of borderline states: "What castration anxiety is to neurosis, separation anxiety would seem to be to borderline states. You could say that for the feminine dimension, anxiety over penetration in neurosis corresponds to anxiety about intrusion in borderline states." [Green 1999: 40] "Something is evacuated into the soma or is acted out!" [ibid.: 41]. There are issues involving splitting (in the Kleinian sense of the term, Green adds) which "may concern various entities or various sectors – psyche/soma, bisexuality (masculine/feminine), thoughts/acts, etc." [ibid.: 41]. In such patients, "the mental apparatus is not an apparatus that simply processes, it is not an apparatus that limits itself to repressing, because repressing implies preserving. It is also an apparatus that, through denial, foreclosure [*forclusion*], and

splitting, evacuates and eliminates – and, in so doing, mutilates itself."
[ibid.: 44]. "[…] there is something else that replaces desire" [ibid.: 45].
The analyst "is always completely at a loss. Why? Because what we are
dealing with is not a form of repression, since the amnesia that we
come up against with such patients corresponds to a complete eradi-
cation of memories, amounting, I would say, to the memory going
blank in all important areas." [ibid.: 55]

If we go back to what I was saying earlier, we can recognize in this
description my hypothesis concerning the way transsexuals function
(I did not mention separation anxiety, although several writers –
Robert Stoller, Susan Coates and Ethel Person [1985], Adam Limentani
[1979] – claim that it is an important factor for transsexuals). However,
two fundamental differences exist between, on the one hand, the
patients with "non-neurotic organizations" whom Green has in
treatment and, on the other, transsexuals:

1) Green's patients are *asking* for analysis (or psychoanalytic help
   of some kind); some even have several successive analyses and
   continue for some years the treatment they have initiated.
   Transsexuals do not do this.

2) The "madness" of Green's patients remains "private" in nature,
   which is not the case of people who are asking for hormonal
   and surgical sex reassignment; *their* madness involves their
   circle of family and friends as well as the physicians who are
   treating them.

I have written elsewhere that transsexualism is a "narcissistic disorder". This is obvious (and it is not an insult, as some transsexuals
have thought): such patients construct their Self – their feeling of
"existing", of "being" – at the cost of adopting the opposite gender
identity. If other people do not enter into their belief system, this
represents a threat to their very being. They are so busy struggling to
maintain their feeling of existing that they cannot pay attention to what
they are making the doctor experience: in other words, they are not at
all ready for analysis of the transference. A male analyst who has a
male-to-female transsexual patient in analysis (it can happen, though it
rarely does; there has been just one example in our Unit), will really be
put to the test: for his patient, he does not exist as a human being with
feelings, and he will be incessantly confronted with the patient's desire
to be rid of his penis – thereby reactivating, in the analyst, the castration anxiety that the patient does not feel. The situation is different for
a female analyst whose patient is a woman who wants her breasts

removed; the analyst will be appalled, she will seek support from her own erotic and maternal experience of the breast, and feel just how much the patient's inability to have an erotic experience of the breast has to do with a poor relationship with the maternal breast.

Of course, some of my colleagues do argue that transsexualism is a psychosis. [In particular, Lacanian psychoanalysts. Cf. the two volumes edited by Czermak and Frignet (1997).] The approximately 3% of those who ask for hormonal and surgical sex reassignment are presented by these writers as typical of all transsexuals. They are entitled to their opinion, but not to attribute it – as they do – to Stoller. At no time did Stoller ever write that transsexuals were psychotic; indeed he argued energetically for the opposite point of view and went as far as to say that describing true transsexuals as "psychotic" was tantamount to prostituting the latter term. For Stoller, when male-to-female transsexuals claim that they are women, they are telling the truth about their primary experience of identifying with their mother: this is not a delusion; it is an illusion.

Indeed, in transsexuals there is no manifestly overwhelming delusion, with hallucinations, intense anxiety of what is called the archaic type, or loss of the sense of reality. At the most, we could perhaps be inclined to talk of an "encapsulated delusion" when the patient says that his phalloplasty (a false penis) is proof of the veracity of his claim that he is a man. It is even more subtle than that: he needs to have the support of a perception in order to deal with what the "missing" object could trigger off inside him – not castration anxiety, but annihilation anxiety. For such a patient, it is existentially vital that he be a man; otherwise he is nothing at all.

It could then be suggested that transsexualism is a defence against psychosis. I have met a few transsexuals who wanted not to be a man or a woman, but to replace the brother or sister who had died before the patient was born. Child psychiatrists are very familiar with the issues involved in the "substitute child" situation which leads to psychosis. For transsexuals, such a substitution is actually desired; it is experienced as a mission, not as something they have to submit to – and that defence against psychosis is really quite successful.

Of course, transsexualism is not a neurosis, even though there may be in the patient neurotic mechanisms and aspects which could prove supportive if psychotherapy were to be undertaken. That said, producing mental representations is not an easy task, and the results are relatively poor. As Green says: "Something is evacuated into the soma or is acted out". [Green 1999: 41]

Evacuation into the soma could well make us think of *anorexia nervosa* in adolescence. In 90–95% of cases this disorder involves adolescent girls, while over the years it was thought that there were three or four male-to-female transsexuals for every female-to-male (there is, it would seem, a recent trend towards uniformity). The anorexic patient weighing 4.75 stones claims she is fat, while the transsexual says that (s)he is a woman with a male body or a man with a female body. I have seen in consultation some patients who suffered from *anorexia nervosa* and were at the same time transsexual.

Splitting and denial would make us think not only of psychosis but also of perversion – though perversion would perhaps tend to evoke the fetishist transvestite.

When I began my training as a psychiatrist, what a surprise it was for me to discover that, contrary to what we usually believe, a mad person is never completely mad – as the Kleinians would put it, there are healthy aspects and ill ones, psychotic ones; others would say that there are neurotic mechanisms and psychotic ones. When I read Freud and began my training as a psychoanalyst, I realized that we are all a bit mad somewhere, that we all have mechanisms and aspects which are neurotic and psychotic. It is not a question of the healthy individual on the one hand (the psychiatrist!) and, on the other, the "insane" or "mentally disturbed" person (the one who consults the psychiatrist); it all has to do with quantity and possible resistance to mobilization. When I first began to see transsexuals in my consultancy, my feeling was that these were people who were extremely unhappy (as Harry Benjamin put it: "Transsexuals are amongst the unhappiest people I have ever met"); sometimes, but not always, I have managed to dialogue with them on equal terms. This does not, however, modify my opinion that the very idea of changing one's sex is a mad idea.

Chapter Six

Masculinity and femininity

I t is time to address the fundamental issue concerning what masculinity and femininity really are. If we ask a transsexual, for whom
the question of being acknowledged as a man or as a woman is of
vital importance, what a man or a woman is, the answer we obtain will
be remarkable for its sheer poverty. Transsexuals are not inclined to
write essays on the topic, and often the answer will be a mere "It's
what I am" – whereas, for the observer, it is precisely what he or she is
not ... If they do elaborate on their answer, transsexuals fall back on the
social stereotypes prevalent in their culture.

The distinction between the two dimensions male/female and
masculine/feminine is very important, but is not always easy to
express; it depends on the language that we use. In English, for
example, there is no problem, just as the difference between "sex" and
"gender" is easy to express.

I. Male or female

It was to some extent as a result of the invention of gender that it
became obvious that the male/female dimension had to be differenti-
ated from the masculine/feminine one. One's sex is male or female –
this is a biological matter – whereas one's gender is masculine or
feminine – a social and psychological matter, the psychological aspect
being fundamentally influenced by social factors, with little heed for
biology. The differences between male human beings and female
human beings are universal; the same is not true of those between
masculine and feminine.

Neither of these two dimensions can be reduced to contrasting pairs.
In France, as in many other countries, regulations concerning civil

status know of only two sexes. In reality, however, though human beings tend to present all the characteristic features of one sex or the other, in 1.7% of births there is an "in-between" state. In order to avoid dichotomy, Anne Fausto-Sterling speaks of a *continuum*; but it is not a continuum: there are no quantitative variations, nor can all possible cases be categorized in some kind of periodic table, as Melicow has attempted to do. Between the all-male and the all-female there are several possible scenarios in which we find combinations of chromosomal formula (XXY Klinefelter's syndrome; XO Turner's syndrome), the presence or absence of gonads (Turner's syndrome), type of gonads (testicles, ovaries, ovotestes), hormone dosage and response to hormones, nature of the internal genital organs and appearance of the external genitalia.

Intersexed does not mean belonging to both sexes. For Freud, all human beings possess features that belong to both sexes; he argued that the terms "man" and "woman" are mere abstractions. Perhaps we should turn that idea on its head: "men" and "women" exist, while the idea of "human beings" is an abstract one. In Freud's view, bisexuality (it would be better were we to use a neologism such as "bisexuation", "bi-sexed disposition") was based on embryological considerations. At the very beginning of gestation, there are both Wolffian and Müllerian ducts in all embryos; in the future female, the Wolffian ducts regress, as do the Müllerian ducts in the future male; they remain in vestigial form in each case. In addition Freud saw the clitoris as an aborted penis: in other words as a male organ. The primary state of being was male in all cases, with women possessing genital organs of both sexes – a male clitoris and a female vagina and vulva; women were therefore more bi-sexed in nature than men. Nowadays, however, we know that if there is no active intervention by androgens and antimüllerian hormones at seven weeks of gestation, the embryo will develop into a female organism in spite of having an XY chromosome formula. The primary state of being would therefore seem to be female. It could be argued, then, that the penis is a hypertrophied and androgenized clitoris ... It would, however, be more reasonable to say that there is an absence of differentiation *ab origine*, with a double potentiality. In any case, it is not the manner in which the embryo develops which creates a man (or a woman); society does this. Embryo growth creates a male or a female being, and not always consistently at that.

Civil status regulations do not refer to "gender" but to "sex", though they put it thus: masculine or feminine sex. For many years, registering a new-born's sex in civil status records was carried out on the basis of a declaration that on such-and-such a date a child of such-and-such sex was born to so-and-so, the parents, without having to bring any proof of such a statement (nowadays a medical certificate is required). According to the principle of inalienability of civil status, no-one could thereafter change his or her sex; only clerical errors could be corrected. Yet the circumstances in which such a declaration was registered – a decision that would prove decisive for the person's whole life – left much to be desired.

As I have stated, the decision as to whether a new-born child is male or female, and the subsequent declaration as to masculine or feminine sex, is based on the appearance of the infant's external genitalia. In the vocabulary of differences between sex and gender, we could say that a sex (determination of genital organs) is attributed to the individual, and from this his or her gender is derived (attribution of social status, expected behaviour, the feeling of self-identity which is supposed to develop). However, many of those who employ the idea of gender argue in favour of a hiatus between sex and gender, a hiatus that I find unfortunate.

For my part, I would distinguish three levels: the biological one, with the attendant events which occur in the body as such; the social one, with its concomitant expectations as regards the individual; and the psychological one, with the manner in which the individual integrates his or her bodily experiences, other people's attitudes and society's demands, thereby creating a personal sense of self-identity. Although I would have preferred to use the term "sexed identity" – *sexed*, because it refers to sexuation, the division of the human species into two sexes (plus the intersexed), the hallowed expression in English is gender identity. I would not in any case have used the traditional term "sexual identity", so as to be able to reserve the adjective *sexual* for describing matters concerning sexuality, intercourse between the sexes and sexual relations. It should be pointed out that one's sexual preference does not necessarily derive *ipso facto* from one's gender identity, as is often thought to be the case: men are not always gynaecophile, women are not always androphile. Does a homosexual preference derive from "gender identity disorder"? Should sexual preference be considered as an identity?

When the appearance of the genitalia is at variance with other biological components of maleness or femaleness, does one or other of these components carry more weight than the rest? How is the question to be decided? Who should take the decision: the doctor, the parents, the individual directly involved (later on in life, of course)?

Ever since we discovered the existence of chromosomes, the difference between the male formula (XY) and the female one (XX), and the part played by the genes carried by the chromosomes (each encoded for a protein and decisive for development), we have tended to give pride of place to chromosomes in determining a person's sex. For years, the judges of the *Cour de Cassation* refused transsexuals the right to have their civil status records altered because their chromosome formula had not changed.

So, penis or chromosomes? The role played by the penis was the essential factor for Freud, to such an extent that the opposition between men and women was based on the presence or absence of a penis; Freud suggested that women could be thought of as being castrated men. When, one day, one of my woman patients, who, thanks to her past history, was an excellent illustration of Freud's theories on penis envy in young girls, met a male-to-female transsexual, she realized that a woman was quite different from a castrated man and that one does not become a woman by the simple fact of being castrated. I once wrote that transsexuals are guilty of the crime of lèse-Freud because they loathe their penis and demand to have it removed.

Freud spoke as though being a woman was merely negative in content, as though women did not have their own sex organs, as though they were characterized by the simple fact of not possessing the only organ that mattered, as though they were nothing more than a hole (but thereby mysterious and disquieting). His theories were part of an almost universal tradition in which women were debased, even though on a personal level he had a great deal of respect for some intellectual women and did not close the door to psychoanalytic training on them. True, little girls do not have much to show off in the way of a penis; they have internal organs only (and the exact nature of the sensations a girl derives from them remains a moot point) or ones that will develop only later in life (breasts). But women have the capacity to give birth; men do not. Without women, men would have no descendants (Françoise Héritier [2002] emphasizes in particular the woman's capacity to give birth to male children); envy of that particular capacity which women have, added to the need to sever the link which made them so dependent on their mother, means that men defensively overvalue their penis, turning it into a *phallus*, the symbol of narcissistic completeness.

Can a man who does not possess a penis still be considered to be a man? Other people may well not consider him to be a man – men, since he is not one of them; women, for whom the capacity to penetrate them is proof of manliness. But experience teaches us that a boy born without a penis can think of himself as a man, even though he may well have to cope with many trials and tribulations on the way, and he may manage to find himself a woman partner.

Can a woman who does not have a vagina think of herself as a woman? Stoller wrote: "If Freud had worked with a woman without a vagina, I think he would have seen that the only thing a woman wants more than a penis is a vagina." [1968: 51] It is, however, easier to construct a neo-vagina than it is to fabricate a neo-penis.

Is a man without testicles still a man, a woman without ovaries still a woman? Their entire hormonal functions will be disrupted and they will undoubtedly be sterile. Many human beings feel badly affected in their self-esteem by the fact that they are sterile, and in some societies they are treated as outcasts. It should be borne in mind that, in cases of sterility, it was always the woman who was thought responsible – the idea that the male member of a couple may have some involvement in their infertility is a comparatively recent one.

Hormones and the sensitivity of tissue receptors to hormones are also very important. As I have pointed out, without androgens and in the absence of an antimüllerian factor, there can be no development of males. I should add that, if the appropriate receptors are not sensitive enough, these hormones will have no effect; this is what happens in cases of androgen insensitivity syndrome, where the genital organs are apparently those of a woman and the testicles secrete oestrogens at puberty, thereby causing breasts to develop. For this reason, the syndrome has been called "testicular feminization".

Every one of the biological components is important. Which of them should be given most weight in determining a person's identity? Traditionally all societies have based that decision on the appearance of the external genitalia, hence the proposal put forward by Money, inter alios: if there is a problem, choose the sex which will be easier to reconstruct – and begin the process of reconstruction as soon as possible. As I have already stated, this attitude is nowadays being somewhat called into question.

In any case, the choice of assigned sex must go hand in hand with a firm conviction on the part of the parents on how they should target the way in which they bring their child up, so that he or she may build up a sense of self-identity that is in harmony with that assigned sex. It may be that the other biological components of sex become so powerful that they represent a real challenge to the child's assigned sex, although this does not happen in the majority of cases. I have already mentioned the experience of John-Joan. Michel Foucault wrote a book [1978 (1980)] which made Herculine Barbin famous; labelled a girl at birth in 1838, she felt attracted to girls at adolescence and was then discovered to be a boy with genital ambiguity; Adelaide Herculine Barbin, nicknamed Alexina, became Abel Barbin for the civil status records in 1860, before she committed suicide in 1868.

II. Masculine or feminine

Some of my colleagues feel that there are indications in Freud's writings concerning gender, i.e. masculine and feminine. I think they are mistaken. The German language gave Freud no grounds for distinguishing between sex and gender; the same word carries the meaning both of "sex" and of "gender" (including "gender" as a grammatical concept) – *Geschlecht*. Similarly, there is only one adjective for "male" and "masculine" – *männlich* – as there is for "female" and 'feminine' – *weiblich*. In any case, Freud had no intention of defining masculine and feminine; in his view, they were directly related to the sex organs and even to the sex cells (spermatozoid and ovum). On that basis, he was able to draw a parallel between masculine and active, feminine and passive (or active with passive aims). He put aside all other considerations, issues concerning the psychological domain, as being conventional or dependent on individual variations:

> A little girl is as a rule less aggressive, defiant and self-sufficient; she seems to have a greater need for being shown affection and on that account to be more dependent and pliant. It is probably only as a result of this pliancy that she can be taught more easily and quicker to control her excretions [...]. One gets an impression, too, that little girls are more intelligent and livelier than boys of the same age; they go out more to meet the external world [...]. These sexual differences are not, however, of great consequence: they can be outweighed by individual variations. [Freud 1933a: 117]

Freud even goes as far as to say that, until puberty, "the little girl is a little man" [ibid.: 118]. He was not blind as to the nature of little girls – the extract I have just quoted is ample proof of that – but questions of what we call gender and gender identity were not an issue for him: his concern was with sex and sexuality. Clitoridal masturbation is a masculine masturbation because the clitoris is an aborted penis; it hardly matters if girls practise other forms of masturbation, some of

which Freud himself described (for example, by using their thigh mus-
cles without manipulating their clitoris). In order to become a woman,
vaginal sensitivity has to be aroused; for Freud, this could not occur in
childhood.

It has been suggested that it was Margaret Mead who invented the
idea of gender, but in her writings she uses systematically the word
"sex". In her book *Male and Female: A Study of the Sexes in a Changing
World*, written in 1948 but remarkably modern in its outlook, she
pointed out that the conception of what is masculine on the one hand
and feminine on the other is not universal – it varies according to the
society in which one lives – and that the ways in which any given culture raises and educates its children aim to ensure that males are
masculine and females feminine in accordance with the social criteria
of masculinity and femininity as that society defines them. Any given
psychological feature, task or adornment will be masculine in one
society and feminine in another, except for war (and even here women
have fought wars, a phenomenon which is becoming increasingly frequent) and for motherhood (though some men practise the *couvade* or
sympathetic pregnancy, a set of rituals in which they experience the
throes of childbirth!)

In order to be acknowledged as a man, one has simultaneously to be
male and comply at least partly with the masculine criteria of the given
society; in order to be acknowledged as a woman, one has to be female
and comply at least partly with the feminine criteria of that society.
What becomes of those who are "betwixt and between" male and
female? Does society decide, or the individual him- or herself? The
intersexed make this decision (when they are allowed to do so) based
on criteria the existence of which is already acknowledged in the
society; transsexuals base their decision on their experience of themselves, although this has no "objective" basis in the eyes of society,
at least for the time being. Yet the inner constraint which drives transsexuals is not the result of free will or choice, even though they
single-mindedly strive towards the achievement of this project.

Would the creation of an intermediate status – a third sex/gender or,
better, third sexes/genders – resolve these problems? Or is it not rather
the case that the persons concerned want to be accepted as belonging
to one or other of the existing sexes, as men or women, without being
stigmatized because they do not satisfy all the criteria for being male
or female?

The failure to satisfy completely the criteria of the culture in which
one lives does not imply a refusal of one's assigned sex. People may

accept their sex, yet challenge society's interpretations of the characteristic features held to derive from the fact of being male or female.
Freud's epigones, more than Freud himself, have declared that a
woman's wish for a professional career, for example, is tantamount to
phallic striving; some even have gone as far as to write that women,
normally passive, are active when mothering their infant child – in
other words, as mothers, women are virile! It would be difficult to find
a better example of how making dogmas out of theoretical hypotheses
leads only to nonsense. Women must arouse terrible fears and
considerable envy if the result is the trilogy: women are passive,
masochistic and narcissistic. I shall not even mention the fact that they
do not have a superego strong enough to enable them to be creative,
have moral standards, etc.

If the feminist movement had not existed, the life that we women,
living in the Western world at the dawn of the twenty-first century,
lead would be very different from what it is; for a start, I would not be
writing this book.

The transsexual's difficulty in defining masculinity and femininity is
understandable. What transsexuals want is something radically different, and that is what we must try to define. Generally speaking, they
do not have the freedom to think about and to criticize the ideological
aspects of the problem. What really matters to them is to be accepted
as women or men in their own culture. It was only very recently that I
met male-to-female transsexuals who declared that they were feminist;
all those whom I had met previously adopted as an ideal in life for
women what feminists have struggled against with all the strength
they have been able to muster (I even used the term "lèse-feminism"):
"I'll stay at home and do the cooking, I'll take my [adopted] child out
in the pram ..." In order to be accepted, one has to conform, and even
be conformist; there is no sense in adding another reason for potential
rejection to the enormous problem with which they have already to
cope.

Every society aims to define what it means by masculine and feminine. What is attributable to the fact of being male or female is limited
to the position adopted in coitus, to the role each plays in procreation
and to the characteristic features of the psycho-sexual cycle in each sex.
Men penetrate, women are penetrated; men beget, women give birth.
In each case it is one or the other. Psychological characteristics, however, are not all-or-nothing: they are distributed along bell-shaped
curves which overlap, with greater variance within a given sex than
between the sexes. The book written in 1974 by Eleanor Maccoby and

Carol Jacklin reviews a considerable number of studies and is still a work of reference in spite of the criticisms periodically levelled against it. Their conclusion is that there are only four domains in which real differences can be proved: women score higher in language development, men on visual-spatial aptitudes, mathematics, and – though I would hesitate to see this as an advantage – in aggressiveness.

This is not difficult to confirm. Language development in girls begins earlier than in boys, and they score higher on certain verbal tests. Girls evidence lower levels of speech disorder (the overall sex ratio G/B is 2.5): there are four boys who stammer for every girl (a fact already known in ancient times). When the left hemisphere is damaged in some way, aphasia occurs three times more often in men than it does in women. This may have something to do with the way left and right hemispheres operate in the brain – lateral dominance in men is more pronounced than in women.

Men are said to perform better on visual-spatial tests. For mathematics, the cultural environment probably plays a part, as Christian Baudelot and Roger Establet have shown in their book *Allez les Filles!* [1992].

Higher levels of aggressiveness in boys can be observed from early in life. In adulthood there are more men than women in prison, and more murders are committed by men than by women. In *The Second Sex*, Simone de Beauvoir [1949] mentions on several occasions men's greater muscular strength.

These are simply statistical differences. Some girls do have speech problems; some boys are weak in mathematics; there are women murderers, etc. None of these features is characteristic of men or of women as such.

In the nineteenth century it was thought that a girl's brain was not conducive to her learning Latin; in the twentieth century that it prevented her from learning mathematics ... In the twenty-first century, it now has to be admitted that girls learn to read more easily than boys do, and that they are higher achievers than boys at all levels during their schooling – in fact, it is only at university level that boys overtake girls: young women at that age have other concerns such as finding a partner and having children, and these sometimes divert their attention from their studies and their careers. Women have specific guilt feelings about achieving success both in what men cannot do as well as in what they can – about accomplishing what civilization has hitherto declared to be masculine as well as what it deems to be feminine.

III. What do transsexuals refuse?

Some women loathe their periods ("Thank heavens! That's me post-menopausal!" one of my patients wrote to me recently); some do not want to have children; some suffer from penis envy all their life – but they have no difficulty in seeing themselves as women. Some women's object choice is homosexual or bisexual – but they have no difficulty in seeing themselves as women. There are feminist militants who fight for equality of rights as between men and women, equal opportunity in politics, etc. – but they have no difficulty in seeing themselves as women.

Some men have likings for activities that our culture calls feminine; some feel themselves to be tender and intuitive; some look after babies ("modern" fathers) – they have no difficulty in seeing themselves as men. There are virile homosexuals and effeminate homosexuals, but they all see themselves as men.

What do transsexuals refuse? Maleness, masculine status? Female-ness, feminine status?

When the refusal in boys begins as early as the end of the first year of life, social status can hardly be a factor; it would therefore seem to be the case that the child's maleness as such is being rejected. What does he perceive of his maleness? A certain kind of muscular tonicity, his penis ... But he does not know that other human beings have different bodily feelings and that these other human beings are girls. When he adopts certain forms of behaviour, is this due to some message or other from his brain or has it to do with the fact that his parents reinforce certain traits negatively or positively? Supposing he throws away his toy cars and wants a doll – how is he to know the masculine or feminine connotations of these toys? This cannot be due to the simple workings of a nucleus at the base of his brain, the one which triggers mounting or lordosis in rats; the cortex has a role to play whenever symbolic activity appears. He hardly knows how to walk, yet he wants to wear his mother's high-heeled shoes and put on her necklace. Does he want to be like his mother, as a person to whom he feels particularly attracted? Is this love, merging, fetishistic cathexis of what belongs to her (this idea will later come to mind when, at around four years of age, we see how he caresses his mother's wedding dress or the hair of a Barbie doll)?

Later, he will notice that girls do not have a penis – at about 18 months, infants learn of the anatomical difference between the sexes [Roiphe and Galenson 1981] – and tries to pull his penis off. He may think that it is attached to his body by snap fasteners; sometimes, but this occurs only very rarely, he may try to cut it off. He prays to God to make it disappear. As an adult, he wants to have it removed surgically: "Help me get rid of this piece of meat [sic!] that dangles between my legs and is of no use to me!"

The young boy says: "I would like to have been a girl. I would like to become a girl." The adult man says: "I am a woman." He finds being a man unacceptable. Masturbation makes him feel anxious; he does not wish to have sexual intercourse with a woman. He wants to wear women's clothing with prettier colours; one of my patients feels that he does not have a life, that he has no right to live because he cannot have coffee sitting at a pavement table wearing a nice little flowery skirt. He wants to put on make-up and nail varnish. He wants to be accepted as a woman; he wants other people to call him "Madam"; he wants to be treated as a woman. Deep inside he feels that he *is* a woman, yet he does not know what a woman feels; his organs do not send him the kind of message that a woman receives from her body. After the operation, he said: "I can experience a woman's orgasm now." The inside of his body is not that of a woman. How can he know what a woman's orgasm is like, when even a woman does not know how another woman experiences it?

What is the main issue here: horror of his penis and of the hair on his body ... or the attraction for things feminine as he imagines them to be?

Very feminine-like boys are said to be identified with their mother; Stoller argues that there is nothing conflictual in that identification. In fact, such a boy identifies with an image which he creates of an ideal woman who does not look like his mother. His mother, say, has her hair cut short and wears jeans; the portrait he paints of himself as a girl is that of a beautiful princess with long blonde hair, wearing a full-length dress, and he is fascinated by long dresses that swish and swirl. But he may draw also a picture of a fearsome woman dressed all in black, wearing high-heeled shoes that could stab you to death. Rather than the blissful symbiosis between mother and child that Stoller described when talking of his discussions with and treatment of mothers who have very feminine-like sons, the boy seems to have two conflicting images of women; though he may well have experienced wonderful moments of intimacy with his mother, he may also have had feelings of being smothered, engulfed. Perhaps the best way of breaking free of such a mother is to be a woman oneself, thereby becoming as powerful as she is.

What of girls who reject their assigned sex? They want above all to be acknowledged as men. It all begins early in life, but in a somewhat more subdued manner than in boys, because our culture is intolerant towards boys who behave like girls whereas, nowadays, it is tolerant towards girls who behave like boys: girls may play with toy cars, wear trousers, practise sports ...

Though the feminine-like boy was a pretty baby about whom everyone used to say "Oh, what a lovely little girl you have there!", the masculine-like girl was a bit of a horror: active, agitated and restless. Often her mother would cathect her negatively for a variety of reasons (depression, illness). She felt herself ill-accepted as a girl, and faced with a wholly negative representation of femininity. One of my patients did not think that the facial malformation which afflicted her could have played any part in her experience of life, until the moment she told me that, from the day she was born, her family referred to her as "the monster"; even though she knew this – i.e. just how much femininity was looked down on by everyone in her family – it was not enough to rid her of the impossibility she felt of accepting herself as a woman, so deeply was what she had experienced in the first months and years of her life imprinted on her.

When the girl's breasts develop, they will be vehemently rejected, not because of the sensations they arouse, but because they are what designate her – denounce her – as a woman. "Breasts, how awful!" Periods will be very difficult to cope with, but less so than breasts; periods are not what one notices first, and they can quite easily be hidden from view.

Does she want a penis, whatever the price to pay? Is female-to-male transsexualism the extreme form of penis envy? No. Of course female-to-male transsexuals would like to have a functional penis; but given the meagre results and the complications that phalloplasty entails, female-to-male transsexuals often abandon the idea of having this done, preferring to wait until more progress has been made in surgical procedures. I have met only one transsexual for whom the ability to penetrate his woman partner with a part of his body was so important that he risked his life by undergoing a procedure which enabled him to have a sufficiently inflexible phalloplasty. That patient himself would say: "It goes beyond transsexualism. I don't understand it. I obtained the change in my identity, I live as a man, I'm happy. Yet, I absolutely have to penetrate my partner." A word in passing: Belgium is, to my knowledge, the only country which demands phalloplasty before granting a woman any change in civil status.

To be able to live as a woman (or as a man) seems therefore to be of paramount importance. What is nowadays called transgenderism would allow for a change in gender without any physical transformation. On the one hand, more often than not, there is no legal provision for changing one's civil status when one is still capable of procreating as a member of one's original sex. In addition, not every transsexual would be happy with such a state of affairs; changing the appearance of their body, which, for them, is tantamount to changing their body as such, is a key factor. They argue that it is not the sex of the body that determines one's identity, but the sex of the soul – yet at the same time they want a physical, bodily trace of their change of identity, because biological factors have such a powerful influence in contemporary society, to the detriment of symbolic factors and ones which are based on language.

The idea behind transgenderism is, in the end, to do away with the notion of gender altogether; neither birth certificates nor identity papers should carry any mention of gender. The supporters of transgenderism argue that the reasons gender was important for society have almost all disappeared or are about to disappear: military service, the right to vote, legal provisions which treat men and women differently as regards rights of succession, marriage. But there is still the matter of sports competitions! And that of procreation.

The battle fought by homosexuals to obtain the right to marry has been crowned with success in many countries. It could be said that the word "marriage" is no longer meaningful, or that there is no longer any need for what used to be called marriage. In France there is now a contract of mutual help and assistance, the PACS (Civil solidarity pact). All that marriage does is to announce the fact that the two persons involved are in a sexual relationship. In the past, marriage was linked to founding a family by natural means, and therefore could not join together two persons of the same biological sex. Nowadays founding a family is quite commonly practised outside the bonds of matrimony. In addition, founding a family can take place with the help of the *socius* (adoption) or with that of a specific member of the *socius*: the doctor who can help with medically assisted procreation. Divorce is quite a common occurrence, and children have to cope with reconstituted families. Parenthood has become a multiple phenomenon. The three components of parenthood have crystallized and become dissociated: parenthood of the genitors, parenthood of those who actually bring up the children, and legal parenthood which gives rights and imposes duties (with reciprocal obligations on the children involved). Families reconstituted after divorce where there is a claim that recognized status be granted to the step-parents, a request that the secret concerning adoption or sperm donor in cases of insemination be removed – these complex situations demand innovative responses. What are we to do with this initial lack of parenting that becomes transformed into an excessive form? Do the children concerned get what they need out of it?

There are specific problems concerning transsexuals and parenthood: questions which remain, generally speaking, unaddressed. Yet it is quite an issue for a child born before the transformation to see his or her father become a woman (or mother a man). The reaction of the children we have seen in our consultation (children whose fathers are male-to-female transsexuals) is variable and depends on the child's age. As young children, they say: "It's a real father and a false woman; it's our father and we love him", though, for some, it is a tremendous shock. As adolescents, they find it highly embarrassing to introduce themselves to their prospective in-laws as having two mothers and no father. As adults they do not know how to introduce to their children the grandfather who appears to be a woman. After the transformation the transsexual wants to be a parent – but a parent of the opposite sex. Recourse to adoption or to artificial insemination by donor creates problems: there are so few adoptable children and so many candidate parents that it seems preferable to avoid what appears at the very least to be a risk factor; medically assisted procreation is intended for cases of hypo-fertility or infertility for medical reasons (in transsexuals, this condition is not the consequence of any pathological state of their organs; it is due to the surgical procedure, and is therefore iatrogenic). Yet transsexuals have been granted a change in their civil status records, so that all the prerogatives of their new sex are now theoretically open to them; but there is a great deal of reluctance on this issue. Their new identity is not acknowledged as carrying with it the cultural values that correspond to it, or as sufficient for enabling a child to identify satisfactorily with such a parent. Society thus places the transsexual in a quandary.

IV. The sexual difference and sexual equality

As I have pointed out transsexualism is a phenomenon which is quite distinct from any challenge to prevalent conceptions of masculinity and femininity in our contemporary civilization. Feminism is not a form of transsexualism, nor transsexualism a form of feminism.

Some feminists deny that there are differences between the sexes – holding them to be mere inventions of society. Transsexuals emphasize the differences between the sexes – they want simply to be on the other side and have difficulty in putting up with the mixture of masculine and feminine that they feel inside themselves.

It is quite unreasonable to deny the existence of the "sexual difference". Every psychological trait may be present in either of the sexes, as we have just seen. However, certain features are derived from biology, from the physical nature of the body, and they cannot be eliminated. Accepting one's identity as a man or as a woman implies accepting the characteristic features of being male or female. The difference is at its most pronounced in sexual intercourse and procreation, but it exists anyway in the experience one has of one's body and in the psycho-sexual cycle.

Man penetrates, woman is penetrated. No man can bear children or breast-feed them; doses of hormones can trigger the onset of lactation in some men, and intra-peritoneal pregnancies in males have been attempted. These are contrivances, not the ordinary, safe and inexpensive way to breast-feed or to bear children.

Though some aspect or other of being male or female may be rejected, nobody could argue that they do not exist. The intersexed suffer because all the aspects of maleness or femaleness are not present inside them; transsexuals suffer because of the presence of some aspects that run contrary to their proclaimed identity.

Puberty begins earlier in girls and is marked by the onset of their first periods, with the outflow of blood, an event which is much more traumatic than a boy's first ejaculation. Of course, the girl's first periods may not be traumatic if she is prepared for it, if she is proud to be reaching this milestone in life that makes of her a grown-up, a woman. The accounts that Hélène Deutsch gives in her book *The Psychology of Women* [1945] have more to do with the past than with the present, although they did have some impact on Simone de Beauvoir as she was writing *The Second Sex*. But various cultures have made of menstrual blood a powerful and dangerous fluid, linked to fecundity, which can be put to malevolent use. When a woman is having her periods, she has to be isolated, she has to purify herself, etc. Even in our own civilization, there are still traces of ancient beliefs and rituals: for example, some women still believe that they will make a complete mess of the mayonnaise if they try to make it when they are having their periods, or that it is dangerous to go swimming. Women are experienced as having a wound which – periodically – re-opens: on the walls of prehistoric caves, the vulva is represented as a wound and the male sex organ as a weapon with a blade. Maurice Godelier [1982] gives the example of the Baruya, for whom the main task of menstrual blood is to provide irrefutable "proof" of the fact that women are victims of themselves – and of themselves alone. And women can only agree to that. "For indeed a Baruya woman has merely to see the blood start to flow between her thighs for her to hold her tongue and mutely consent to whatever economic, political and psychological oppression she may be subjected" [ibid.: 233]. One of the key words in that quotation is the notion of "consent".

A woman's sexual life is constantly marked by blood: first periods, menstruations, the bleeding which accompanies defloration, the blood of giving birth and the expulsion of the afterbirth and, finally the cessation of blood at menopause. At that point women are sometimes considered to be men.

Various societies have marked out the development of their menfolk, which does not contain such definitive and natural caesurae as for women, by often cruel initiation ceremonies.

The sexual difference has to do with the facts of life. Some have drawn the conclusion that women were thereby proved to be inferior – which is why certain feminists reject the whole idea. But the equality for which all feminists are fighting (and, in that sense, I am a feminist) is on quite a different plane, that of equal rights. Although everything is not perfect, at the dawn of the twenty-first century in France, our situation is really quite a pleasant one. All we have to do is think of the plight of the daughters and wives of those who have immigrated among us, of women in Pakistan, Afghanistan, etc.

The problem of equality of rights as between the sexes is not one which concerns transsexuals. They are fighting for their rights to be acknowledged within their own particular and highly specific difference. In France, changing the civil status records means that, theoretically at least, they have access to all of the prerogatives of their new sex – and to marriage in particular, which is not the case elsewhere. As I have indicated, however, there are still problems relating to the adoption of children and recourse to medically assisted procreation. These are very difficult issues. We may well seem to be contradicting ourselves when, on the one hand, we emphasize the simply palliative and illusory character of hormonal and surgical sex reassignment, while, on the other, we support the transsexuals' claim to have access to all the rights and privileges that their new sex bestows on them. The crucial problem lies in the earlier stage, when it was decided to legitimate sex-change operations. If these are no longer illegal, and if changes to civil status records are permitted, it then follows that the individuals concerned are quite entitled to exercise all the rights appertaining to their newly defined sex – otherwise we are forcing them to live in a no-man's land, subjectively and officially men or women, but objectively and for all practical purposes neither men nor women.

Chapter Seven

The development of gender identity

The intersexed (1.7% of the general population, 3‰ present genital ambiguity) and transsexual individuals (one in every 30 000 to 100 000, depending on the statistics quoted) form only a small proportion of the general population. We can, however, learn much about the development of gender identity by studying them.

I. In the other's mind

Gender identity is usually considered to be a secondary phenomenon, developing in the context of the classic Oedipus complex between three and five years of age, or in the early genital phase (Roiphe and Galenson), i.e. in the second half of the second year of life. That may well involve the individual's representation of what the difference between the sexes actually is, but not his or her feeling of gender identity, which develops earlier. The self is not neuter; it has gender.

A baby (though in some languages the word is grammatically neuter) is never neuter as far as the parents are concerned; and the latter strongly influence the infant's growing awareness of what he or she is. For the parents, their baby began to have a specific gender in their Oedipal dreams as children and adolescents, then again during the mother's pregnancy in their fantasies involving the forthcoming child. (According to Michel Soulé, learning of the baby's sex by means of ultrasound scans is equivalent to a voluntary abortion of fantasy representation, but this is not in fact the case: knowledge of what the scans say does not interrupt fantasy activity. Some parents, however, prefer to remain in the dark and do not wish to be informed of the scan results on this particular point.) The baby is there, and must be either a boy or a girl, not something neuter. Whenever there is any doubt about which sex to attribute to the new-born, such that the doctors request that any decision be postponed until a later date, this is intolerable for the child's parents. [See Anne-Marie Rajon's remarkable article (1988).] The child must be given a name, and choosing a first name which could apply equally well to both sexes [Lee, for instance] does not answer the question asked by family and friends: "A boy or a girl?". Cathecting the child's sex determines a whole series of words, feelings, attitudes and behaviour. From the very beginning of life babies are treated differently according to whether they are girls or boys; much research still has to be done to highlight the actual details of this phenomenon. According to Lézine, Robin and Cortial [1975: 140]: "Any discrepancy between the infant's own rhythm and the mother's facilitating or restricting attitude seems to be more pronounced in the case of girls than in that of boys."

It is of course true that babies experience their bodies differently according to their sex (musculature, genitalia, etc.). But babies do not know that there are other infants, human beings just like they are, who are sexually different and who have different experiences. They do not know that their own experience defines them as a boy or as a girl. The parents know, and they respond by expressing their satisfaction or their displeasure at some particular item of behaviour. Stoller used the term *shaping* to describe what goes on. Depending on the parent's response, the baby may feel comfortable or ill at ease as regards his or her inner feelings or external acts.

Later, when the child discovers that there are other children, children of the opposite sex, that experience will be traumatic – the two emblematic figures of that traumatic discovery are castration anxiety and penis envy. Children react to this by rallying together in same-sex groups as though to corroborate the value of their own particular identity. In nursery school, where all the children are together in class and share in the various activities, a spontaneous form of sex-based segregation takes place in the playground; that is where a long history of mutual disparagement of the opposite sex begins – as well as a somewhat more secret envy of that opposite sex. Though Freud had a lot to say about the young girl's penis envy, he remained more or less silent about the young boy's envy of maternal features. Many three- or four-year-old boys have wept when they learned that they would never be able to carry a baby in their tummy, or that their breasts would never contain milk.

Some children swim against the tide and do not befriend others of their own sex. They want to dress up in clothes that belong to the opposite sex (in nursery or nursery school, they may even steal them); they play with toys which in our culture have distinct opposite-sex connotations (which goes to show that refusing one's sex is not a raw biological fact but is dependent upon the way in which cultural values are decoded), and their playmates belong exclusively to the opposite sex. Such girls like fighting and fierce physical activity, the very things which such boys refuse.

Should this be defined as gender identity disorder, or are we really talking about variations in gender identity? Should they be treated or respected? Some would argue for accepting the child's behaviour (as in the film *Ma Vie en Rose* [*My Life in Pink*]). Others believe on the one hand that such a situation is a cause of distress for the child involved, and not only because of intolerance in the environment, and, on the other, that transsexualism is such a painful condition that everything ought to be done to try to prevent its development. Treating such children implies working both with them and with their parents.

II. Core gender identity and gender identity

Identity is a belief which comes to us from our interpretation of messages communicated by our parents, an interpretation which is, generally speaking, reinforced by the events which take place in our bodies and the attitude of other people towards us. For transsexuals, that belief involves also the kind of interpretation they make of their parents' conscious and unconscious messages; it is as though they could not feel their own continuity, their own *self*, feel loved and able to love, feel themselves to have any personal worth other than as members of the opposite sex. That unshakeable conviction, as it is called, is built up over the years and demands the support of other people similarly convinced, whenever bodily events and the sponta-neous attitude of a unanimous circle of family and friends are found wanting.

In the first three years of life, core gender identity – the feeling that one is male or female – is built up in this way. To all intents and purposes it remains unchanging: no person can be reassigned without his or her consent – an intersexed child who is reassigned without consent will be seriously traumatized, to the extent that psychosis may well ensue.

Thereafter, gender identity develops – the feeling of being masculine or feminine. Being masculine or feminine is always defined with

respect to a given culture, and includes variations, nuances and fluc-
tuations. We are all more or less masculine, more or less feminine – but
not "more or less" male or female (with the exception of the intersexed, but here the difference is qualitative, not quantitative).

Psychic bisexuality is the rule. We all have some features, tastes, and
behaviour attributed by our culture to the opposite sex. We put up with
them, more or less. As we have seen, transsexuals are completely
intolerant towards them.

Until fairly recently, fathers did not bottle-feed their babies or
change nappies, because in so doing they ran the risk of losing some
of their virility. The receptive feminine position, sometimes called passive, is felt as a threat [Schaeffer 1997]. Giving in to tenderness is just
not virile. Boys don't cry.

In our culture women seem to feel that they have to get rid of all
kinds of hair (facial hair, hair under their armpits, on their legs). In
places where forced clitoral excision is practised, it is referred to as
removing a masculine part. A clear, well-structured and cogently
argued speech is thought of as being manly.

Cultural traditions are so embedded in each of us that women have
a specific kind of guilt feeling as regards success in their chosen profession; this inhibits them and, in addition to the obstacles which are
otherwise put in their path, contributes to the fact that they hardly ever
reach the most senior positions. In religions which decree that women
are inferior to men and must submit to their will, most women are convinced that they are indeed inferior beings and accept their
subservience.

To rebel against the fate which cultural tradition has decided upon
is not to refuse one's core gender identity; it is to acknowledge that
anatomy does not decide one's fate, but that *society* has decided that
anatomy seals one's fate.

To rebel is no easy matter. For such a rebellion to gather momentum
and modify the condition of women, a conjunction of several factors
was necessary.

In the first place, the French Revolution called into question all
that concerned the established order of things and traditions deriving
from divine right. True, the Declaration of the Rights of Man and of
the Citizen (26 August 1789) applied only to men (*viri*) and not to
human beings in general (*homines*), in spite of the attempt by Olympe
de Gouges to proclaim a Declaration of the Rights of Woman and of
the Female Citizen in September 1791. With the Napoleonic Code of
1804 (the French Civil Code), once again women found themselves

treated as minors and were legally *incapax*. After the struggles of the suffragettes in Great Britain, it was probably the part played by women in the Resistance movement and the fight of the Free French which led General de Gaulle, after the Liberation, to support the call for women to be given the right to vote. Today, the struggle is for equality: more progress has been made in Quebec, for example, than in France.

Access to education for women developed in stages throughout the nineteenth century. To the parish schools were added local authority ones. Then came secondary education (high schools and colleges for women in 1881), and the founding of the prestigious training college at Sèvres for women teachers in higher education (1883). It was not until 1925 that female students followed the same curriculum as their male counterparts, could sit the Baccalaureate exam and therefore have access to university. Education is a crucial element in women's liberation; the Taliban regime in Afghanistan banned girls from attending school.

The nature of work has changed. According to Aristotle, slavery could be abolished only if the weaver's shuttle went by itself. Not only has this become a fact, but it has also become possible to control the entire manufacturing process from a computer keyboard; for a great number of tasks, physical strength is no longer a requisite.

Women now do work that used to be thought of as masculine. As early as the First World War, women were replacing men in the workplace.

Women can now have access to any profession (the prestigious Ecole Polytechnique, the Armed Forces ...), although they are not very often found in the most senior positions.

Women have benefited from technological progress in other ways, too, housework having become much less of a chore. The washing machine does in an hour and by itself what used to take a whole day in the wash-house, as Zola describes in *Gervaise*. Without a refrigerator, shopping for food was a daily task. It would not be difficult to draw up a long list of what has liberated women. In the old days only the "bourgeois" woman – one who could afford to pay another woman to help her out or to do certain chores for her – could escape domestic slavery. It is of course true that many studies show that women still spend more time than men on household tasks, but nowadays many men think it quite natural for them to participate in housework.

Progress in medical science has brought about a decrease in infant mortality. In order to have the same number of surviving children, two or three, a woman no longer has to spend her whole life going from pregnancy to pregnancy.

Contraceptive methods, which nowadays are the prerogative of women, have drastically changed female sexuality and motherhood – no longer a fate to which one has to submit, becoming pregnant is a choice freely decided upon at a time when a woman is able to accept it. This is a highly important factor – indeed, Françoise Héritier [2002] even goes as far as to claim that it is practically the *only* element to have influenced women's liberation. I would say, however, that it is a factor which reinforces others.

Rights and responsibilities as regards children are now parental and not simply paternal (at one point, fathers had the power of life and death over their children).

In our culture, even if progress still has to be made in some domains, women have become full human beings in their own right. Some may still find it difficult to accept their new status.

As we have seen, however, transsexuals do not try to rid themselves of the social status of their biological sex. If female-to-male transsexuals were inspired by feminist ideas or by penis/phallus envy as a symbol of narcissistic completeness, many more females than males would be asking for hormonal and surgical sex reassignment. This is not the case: males have always outnumbered females in the request for hormonal and surgical sex reassignment, though some levelling-out would seem to be gradually taking shape. For transsexuals, their whole being is involved: their capacity to go on living, their right to life. They want to be in the symbolic *locus* of the opposite sex – in fact, not simply the symbolic *locus*, but the real one. They turn the pretence of their new sex into a symbol *and* into something real. That *locus* is meaningful with respect to the transsexual's mother and father, to their gender identity as each of them experiences it, and to their sexuality; the transsexual does not know that. When he or she discovers it, it is too late – it is impossible for the transsexual to be reconstituted in that identity in a different mode. I have heard adults make the astonishing comment: "If my father and mother started having sexual intercourse again, I would think about abandoning my plans to change my sex."

III. Gender identity and sexual preference

According to John Money, among others, sexual preference is part of an individual's G-I/R [gender-identity/role]: gender identity is the private side, gender role the public one. As I have pointed out, behaviour which does not conform to the stereotypes of the society in which one lives does not necessarily lead to a refusal of one's gender identity. We must now consider the relationship between gender identity and sexual preference.

Homosexuality used to be called "inversion". Some talked of a female brain in a male body, a notion that nowadays is often applied to transsexuals. We now know that some male homosexuals are effeminate, while others are as virile as they come; in some homosexual couples the two partners complement each other, while in others they are surprisingly similar, as if each were the mirror-image of the other. Similarly, female homosexuals are not always virile and many may be perfectly feminine in their appearance.

Animal behaviour is sometimes referred to in this context. But homosexuality in animals is not in any way comparable to that in human beings, where it is an exclusive object choice.

As far as the origins of homosexuality are concerned, the same debate as for transsexualism takes place: biological, psychological, or perhaps more to the point interaction between a given organism and the environment.

However, no-one gives credence to the idea of a transsexual gene, whereas that of "gay" or homosexual genes has been considered: one marker was thought to have been identified – the extremity of the long arm of the X-chromosome in the Xq 28 region. That said, genes are now thought to predispose an individual towards a particular sexual preference rather than to determine such an option. It has to be remembered that genes code for proteins, and not directly for behaviour, still less for complex feelings, which have many and various cultural components.

Does homosexuality involve gender identity disorder or is it a variation on gender identity? For Elizabeth Moberly [1983], transsexualism is the extreme form of homosexuality. In both cases there is a deficit in the attachment relationship to and identification with the same-sex parent. The quest for an erotic relationship with someone of the same sex derives from the need to make up for that deficit, and includes the desire for love and tenderness. Moberly's argument is quite subtle: she does not say that the same-sex parent was inadequate or absent, but that he or she was experienced as such by the child. As regards male-to-female transsexualism, Stoller claimed that there was too much mother and not enough father, whereas in cases of female-to-male transsexualism there was too much father and not enough mother.

Moberly's hypothesis would seem to be firmly based on clinical data. Although I do not have the same clinical experience in cases of homosexuality as I have with transsexuals, I would say that the homosexuals who have consulted me did indeed suffer from the relationship and identificatory deficiency as regards the same-sex parent that she describes (but not all those who suffer from a relationship and identificatory deficiency with the same-sex parent become homosexual). Anyway, psychoanalysts can discuss only a limited form of homosexuality: the only homosexuals who consult a psychoanalyst are those for whom their homosexuality is a problem or those who, for some reason or other, have a breakdown; those homosexuals who are comfortable with their homosexuality do not consult a psychoanalyst. Like homosexuals, transsexuals do not see themselves as mentally ill – but they do need to consult a physician if they are to obtain the physical transformation they want.

As I have pointed out, transsexuals do not see themselves as homosexuals when they are attracted to people who are of the same biological sex as they are, because, in their view, their biological sex does not define their identity: they are, therefore, heterosexual. The only transsexuals who see themselves as homosexual are those who, after surgery, are attracted to people of the same sex as their target sex; this is a rare occurrence. Most of the transsexuals concerned are transvestites and they call themselves "lesbian".

It is not the refusal of one's assigned sex that leads to homosexuality. It could on the other hand be argued that homosexuality arises from the refusal to acknowledge in the fullest sense of the term the sexual difference, with all the consequences that it entails.

What arouses sexual desire and enables us to obtain erotic satisfaction remains mysterious. Human beings are characterized by the fact that their sexuality is not coupled to the reproductive process nor linked to oestrus. They can copulate outside the period in which they are fecund, with no aim of procreating, simply for pleasure; this opens the door to all sorts of variants, thereby giving rise to the idea that human sexuality is perverse in nature.

Attempts have been made to link these variant forms to biological determination or to childhood experiences. But neither of these hypotheses can fully explain – and even less, modify – all the particular features of the erotic life of each individual, what John Money called "love maps".

Chapter Eight

A testing time for us

T ranssexuals put us to the test. We cannot remain indifferent to
their suffering; nor can we stay aloof as they challenge us with
the question that means so much to them. We respond with our
own subjectivity: to say that any one human being is a man or woman
is initially a statement about surface criteria; conformity to social criteria which vary according to cultural patterns; deep-down
psychological criteria which vary according to the expectations each of
us has.

The various kinds of discourse that surround transsexuals are part
of the diversity of the universe of discourse, in which, whatever our
willingness to do so, we can never find common ground. We have no
choice but to make a personal choice.

We have to hold on to reliable points of reference and, in spite of our
compassion, we must not lose the "sex compass" – in other words,
unqualified acknowledgement of the sexual difference (which constitutes one of the aspects of human finitude), the acceptance of that
difference and the ability to make that "raw" biological fact meaningful
in our life as human beings.

At every moment our counter-transference is mobilized. All those
who have worked with transsexuals say that finding a common
language is very difficult; the dilemma is how to hold on to what and
who we are while remaining sensitive to this strange difference.

I. The universe of discourse and its diversity

It is not easy to talk to a transsexual who, instead of saying "I wonder
if …", states quite plainly, "I am a member of the opposite sex". If the
person concerned does not look like a member of the opposite sex, does

not have the identity papers of someone of the opposite sex, if he or she is not convinced – nor convincing – as to the irrevocability of their decision (some patients, after a sex-change operation, ask for their original sex to be restored to them – and some even go as far as to nullify this second sex change in order to recover the outcome of the first sex-change procedure), what are we doing if we address the person as if he or she were in fact a member of the opposite sex? We would be agreeing wholeheartedly with the request, and giving up any idea of exploring the situation together. Transsexuals sometimes find our non-committal stance offensive. Yet they, too, still tend to hesitate as to grammatical gender when they talk about themselves; this disappears later, once they come fully to terms with themselves as regards their decision.

Psychoanalysts like to adopt an attitude of benevolent neutrality. But the French language does not possess a neuter gender; and even in those languages which do have one, those in which the adjective does not agree in gender with the noun, the problem still cannot be side-stepped. In French it is just not possible to choose on each and every occasion "innocuous" words such as "young" ["*jeune*" – the masculine and feminine forms have identical spelling] rather than "little", etc. ["*petit(e)*" – the two forms are spelt differently, the feminine form taking the final "e"]. When we have to write to the patient, what form of address should be used on the envelope (what does his or her immediate circle know about the situation?) and as an introductory greeting in the letter itself? I decided at one point to explain my standpoint as clearly as possible: I tell the person consulting that I have no intention of being offensive but that, for the time being and until the sex change has been carried out, I shall continue to use the form of address corresponding to his or her original sex. Sometimes, once we get to know each other better, I ask the patient what form of address he or she would prefer me to use; to my surprise, some patients have replied: "With you, it doesn't matter" – with me, the dice are loaded, I know what it is all about. The important thing is that strangers spontaneously attribute to the transsexual patient his or her target gender.

When writing about transsexuals, physicians in France have attempted to use the masculine form of the word for male transsexuals [*transsexuel*] and the feminine form for female transsexuals [*transsexuelle*]. Transsexuals themselves, however, object to this and make the opposite choice: since male transsexuals are, in their own eyes, women, they use the feminine form, while female transsexuals use the masculine form. This of course makes it impossible to use the masculine/ feminine dichotomy in the form of words used, since no-one would know to which kind of transsexuals we are referring. In order to make this clear and to show consideration for the patient's sensitivity, it has therefore become customary to use the terms male-to-female and female-to-male transsexual (in abbreviated form, MTF and FTM). The direction in which the transformation has taken place is used to differentiate between the cases.

All these precautions only go to emphasize how awkward it is to adopt fully the patient's perspective and to see the situation through his or her eyes, as a woman or as a man; patients are sharply critical of our discomfort. Simply for the patient to say that he or she is a woman or a man and for us to go along with that does not make the problem go away: the transsexual is not a woman who was born female nor a man who was born male, and will come up against problems that no-one has the power to prevent.

Militant groups act as though everything becomes self-evident as soon as a person says with conviction, "I have not *become* a woman, I have always been one" – even though her appearance may sometimes have a grotesque quality to it that contradicts her claim. "I have not changed my sex or my gender. I am at long last what I have always been: I am me." In these militant groups, it is possible to obtain hormones without a proper detailed medical check-up; people are encouraged to demand surgery; details of contacts in foreign countries are handed out – and catastrophe ensues when operations are carried out with no previous case supervision.

Some physicians in foreign countries have turned transsexualism into a source of income. They present their results in shows worthy of television programmes: before-and-after photographs of noses and breasts which bear witness to the miracle that is "cosmetic" surgery; then they show faces and bodies, the most beautiful and the most feminine of which is that of the transsexual and not of the woman-born-a-woman. They satisfy the expectations of those who say: "I will be the most beautiful woman of all." Recently operated patients come on to the stage in order to proclaim how happy they are and how wonderful their surgeon is.

Listening to such discourses takes us into the kinds of universe which cannot communicate with each other and that have no truck with our earnest attempts to think through the issues involved.

II. The sex compass and compassion

Physicians who propose hormonal and surgical sex reassignment do so out of compassion. Transsexuals are deeply distressed, and their request is not a passing whim. While psychotherapy does not make them change their minds, the medical profession offers a remedy which is meant to bring some relief to the patients concerned, even though it is illusory: nobody can change his or her sex – sex is not an opinion, it is a reality.

Although the condition cannot be cured, the patient's distress can be relieved to some extent. Long-term outcome research tends to confirm the fact that prescribing physicians are correct in this approach. As I have mentioned, these studies may be far from perfect and leave aside those who have been operated on in "commercial" circumstances. Few patients regret having had the treatment, in spite of subsequent complications. There is still some distress over the fact that nobody can turn a transsexual into a man-born-male or a woman-born-female, though in general patients are less unhappy than they were before.

There is little hope that advances in surgery will make it possible to change one's entire body, chromosomes and internal organs; anyway, even if this were possible one day, it would not erase the life experience the patient had up until then.

It therefore seems important to devise some effective treatment other than hormonal and surgical sex reassignment, even when this is carried out to the best of his or her ability by a demiurge of a surgeon.

Compassion justifies to some extent the practice of hormonal and surgical sex reassignment, and it plays a part also in the indications for this kind of treatment. Surgeons who claim to operate exclusively on primary transsexuals in fact operate also on those who are obviously not primary transsexuals but who have put themselves into such a state that it becomes vital to help them – and the only way to do this is to carry out the requisite operation.

Compassion should not let us forget the sex compass. Our culture, however, tends to do just that, with the media giving disproportionate attention to sex variants (gender and sexuality), leaving very little room for what most human beings long for. The hostile component of erotic arousal and of creation is manifest and glorified in what they show us. Does this help us to live better, or make us lose our bearings even more? What we are shown may not be the reason for our confusion but a manifestation of it. The frontier between private and public life becomes blurred, to the detriment of our intimacy.

III. Our counter-transference

In our work as psychoanalysts, we make use of our theoretical corpus, but we rely much more fundamentally on what the patient makes us experience, feelings which the patient cannot immediately put into words. The kind of experience that significant persons have given the patient throughout his or her life is passed on to us in this way. The counter-transference is what patients stir up inside us; it comes up against what we are and impacts on the way in which we have managed (or failed to manage) the conflicts that we ourselves have had with significant persons in our own life.

With transsexuals, we have to go beyond the simple: "what a mad idea". Of course they do have a mad idea: they want someone to transform their body, an impossible task. But why do they have such a mad idea?

I have in mind a patient who consulted me relatively late in his life. In our first meeting together, the way in which he told me he was a woman and that he would have to have changes made to his body made me feel disheartened. I could not see the slightest hope of doing any psychological work with him, and I referred him on to a colleague who would prescribe the requisite operation; the patient consulted my colleague, then came back to me because he wanted someone to talk to. I then understood that I had let myself fall into the trap laid by an aspect of this patient which was disconcerting and frightening. This was not due to the fact of his being a caricature of a woman, cross-dressed without any talent at all – he was quite simply nothing, neither man nor woman. In his very presentation, he seemed to repel any relationship whatsoever, yet what he desired above all was to have someone share his life, someone for whom he would really count. At the same time, he maintained that this was impossible. Officially a man, he had no desire to flirt with women. Feeling himself to be a woman, trying as much as he could to be a woman, he could not allow himself to be flirted with – his main argument was that he did not have a vagina, just a penis that he concealed at the cost of much pain to himself.

I asked myself what would be more plausible for him – being a woman or being a man? It was impossible to decide; he was nothing. This was the only way he could express the utter distress he felt at having been treated by his father and by his mother as though he were nothing. He was searching desperately for someone who would be able to listen to and understand him, because his parents, each for different reasons, had always refused to do that when he tried to talk to them. And I had almost missed the fact that I, as a psychoanalyst, was attempting to do just that – to listen to and try to understand him. I had, for once, responded immediately to his manifest request, while the most important part lay elsewhere. That patient moved me tremendously. I managed to rid myself of any desire as regards his identity: I had no desire that he be a man or a woman. I wanted simply to help him recover the feeling that he was someone who had the right to live. And, in fact, I managed to transform his outward appearance. He was aware of that – but it was as though that fact posed a relationship threat to him; he did not feel that he was alive enough not to have to take shelter behind a protective façade, alive enough to be able to share intimacy with another human being.

That patient gave me the courage to go on being a psychoanalyst when faced with transsexuals, something that does not go without saying. Even if the hope that exists with children and some adolescents of changing what they are doing with their life is pretty futile when it comes to adults – unless they are still unsure of who they are – we can offer them a place to talk about it and accompany them in the choice they make of their path in life, whatever that may be.

Conclusion

I n Chapter IV, I quoted Stoller [1968: 247]: "The general rule that applies to the treatment of the transsexual is that no matter what one does – including nothing – it will be wrong." We are anyway downstream and not upstream from decisions which have already been taken as to the legality of sex-change surgery and of modification of civil status. Some pressure groups have succeeded in obtaining the support of European institutions, the accent being put on the respect of one's right of privacy. Those countries which have so far resisted are now coming round: for example, the United Kingdom, which until recently did not allow any modification of one's birth certificate, the argument having been that, since a birth certificate records an event which has already taken place, we cannot turn around and say that what has taken place has not in fact taken place. The result of that position was that transsexuals could never marry since, in Great Britain, marriage between two persons of the same biological sex is prohibited; on the other hand, the United Kingdom is very liberal when it comes to changing one's name, modifications to civil status records, passports, etc.

I have been criticized for saying that hormonal and surgical sex reassignment was a mad response to a mad request. I have no intention of attacking anybody; I accept reality for what it is. Transsexuals who feel that they belong to the opposite sex really are in distress, although the origin of their distress may still be enigmatic. Those transsexuals who think that they will be given (or that they have been given) their "true body", that of the opposite sex, refuse to acknowledge that such a transformation is impossible. Others – though they are few in number – say that they are happy enough to take their place among those of the opposite sex.

Actors are very good at playing the part of, or impersonating, the opposite sex without feeling at all concerned by the problem of transsexualism; the boy in *My Life in Pink* and the girl in *Boys Don't Cry* are good examples of the fact that "appearance" is not sufficient to vouch for identity.

Taking one's place among the opposite sex could be possible without undergoing mutilating surgery. Transsexuals do not feel that reassignment constitutes mutilation – they see it as a "restorative procedure". Yet healthy organs are removed – and in several countries surgeons who carry out this operation have had to negotiate with the legal authorities so as to avoid prosecution. There is an illusion, the creation of a "pseudo-", a fake, a chimera. Some surgeons prefer to carry out the female-to-male sex change in spite of the difficulties and limits of that procedure, because it is creative, whereas transforming a man into a woman consists mainly in removing organs. This clearly shows the "demiurge" ambition of surgery. And we cannot but be struck by the fact that some surgeons spend the whole of their working life doing exclusively transsexual surgery.

The role played by surgery with respect to change in civil status is a matter of some debate. Before the rulings of the *Cour de Cassation* in 1992 accepting changes to civil status records in cases of "the syndrome of transsexualism", some transsexuals had been granted the right to do so by the *Tribunal de Grande Instance* (regional court) or the Court of Appeal, while others had had their case dismissed; whenever the question came before the *Cour de Cassation*, the decision was to refuse any such change. The result was total chaos: in the same month a regional court refused a change of civil status to an applicant because he had had surgery before making his application to the court, while a different court turned down a similar application because the plaintiff had not yet had the operation. Because of the threat of prosecution, one of my French colleagues will carry out the operation only after the patient has obtained the requisite change in civil status: "I operate only on the intersexed, not on transsexuals," he says.

Is surgery a necessary condition for obtaining a change in civil status records? Different countries have different laws on the question. The discourse of transsexuals varies also: some protest against the obligation to undergo the operation, while others protest against the obstacles on the road to the operation, which to them is precious in that it enables them "to harmonize their body with their soul, their identity".

Taking their place among the opposite sex without any actual change of sex was what those who refused to accept their assigned sex did in former times; often this was discovered only after their death. It would seem that more women succeeded in going through life as men – and were even treated as saints for it – than men who lived as women. This brings us to "transgenderism". The term is fairly recent and its meaning still tends to fluctuate somewhat – sometimes it includes transsexuals, transvestites, etc.; at others it refers to those who wish to change their gender and not their sex, which could consist of hormonal treatment without surgery or with only partial surgery (e.g. mastectomy only) and a change of first or given name. The problem of their legal status has still not been decided; in 2001, at the International Congress of Sexology in Paris, an Australian participant declared that change in civil status without any physical transformation is now possible in Australia. It is obviously baffling to think that a man in the eyes of the civil status records might give birth or that a male might officially be the mother of a child born of his sperm. These, however, are issues which concern society, law and culture, whereas the problem we face in cases of transsexualism is of another kind altogether and involves the risky manipulation of the person's body.

Some people are said to be "for" hormonal and surgical sex reassignment; others are said to be "against" it. This is quite plainly an oversimplification. Hormonal and surgical sex reassignment is a fact. We can deplore it or rejoice over it – but the patient who wants it will find it. Who could claim to have the power to have it banned all over the planet? Whose aim is that? But we all need to think about this phenomenon, one example among many of what takes place in contemporary society. To be "against" it would imply demonstrating in our towns and cities, carrying prohibitionist banners and thinking we are fighting the good fight when in fact all we are doing is tilting at windmills. To be unconditionally "for" it would imply allowing anybody who wanted surgery to have it, without further ado; those who support such a stance know absolutely nothing about the issues involved and have never witnessed the disastrous outcome it brings in its wake. Prescribing doctors who are not in it for the money do not take such a decision lightly. No-one should be exempted from having to think about what he or she is doing.

We all have to act in accordance with who and what we are. We can agree to listen to transsexuals in our role as psychoanalysts, with the express proviso that we will not in any way participate in the decision as regards hormonal and surgical sex reassignment. To the militant, if we are not "for", we must be "against" – but that is the price to pay for the freedom which opens up the possibility of working things out in our minds.

References

Beauvoir, S. de (1949). *Le Deuxième Sexe*. Paris : Gallimard. [*The Second Sex*. Translated and edited by Parshley, H. M., with an introduction by Crosland, M. New York, Alfred A. Knopf, 1993].

Benjamin, H. (1966). *The Transsexual Phenomenon*. New York: Julian Press.

Baudelot, C. and Establet, R. (1992). *Allez les Filles!* Paris: Le Seuil.

Bradley, S.J., Oliver, G.D., Chernick, A.B. and Zucker, K.J. (1998). "Experiment of nurture: ablatio penis at 2 months, sex reassignment at 7 months, and a psychosexual follow-up in young adulthood". *Pediatrics, 102*, 1, July 1998.

Breton, J., Frohwirth, C., Pottiez, S. and Kindynis, S. (1985). *Le transsexualisme. Étude nosographique et médico-légale*. Paris: Masson.

Chiland, C. (1997). *Changer de sexe*. Paris: Odile Jacob. [*Transsexualism: Illusion and Reality* (translated by Philip Slotkin). London: Continuum; Sage, & Middletown, CT., USA: Weysleyan University Press, 2003.]

— (1999). *Le sexe mène le monde*. Paris: Calmann-Lévy.

— (2003). *Robert Jesse Stoller*. Paris: Presses Universitaires de France.

Chiland, C. and Cordier, B. (2000). *Transsexualisme*. EMC, 37-299-D-20.

Coates, S. and Person, E. S. (1985)."Extreme Boyhood Feminity: Isolated Behavior or Pervasive Disorder?". *Journal of the American Academy of Child Psychiatry, **24**, 6, 702–709.

Colapinto, J. (2000). *As Nature made him*. London: Quartet Books.

Cordier, B., Chiland, C. and Gallarda, T. (2001). "Le transsexualisme, proposition d'un protocole malgré quelques divergences". *Annales médico-psychologiques, **159**, 190–195.

Czermak, M. and Frignet, H. (1997) *Sur l'identité sexuelle*. Paris: Association Freudienne Internationale. Actes des journées du 30 novembre et 1er décembre 1996.

Delcourt M., *Hermaphrodite. Mythes et rites de la bisexualité dans l'antiquité classique*, Paris, PUF, 1958; rééd., 1992, coll. "Dito". [*Hermaphrodite*. (translated by Jennifer Nicholson) London: Studio Books 1961.]

Deutsch, H. (1945). *The Psychology of Women. A Psychoanalytic Interpretation*. New York: Grune and Stratton.

Di Ceglie, D. and Freedman, D. (eds). (1998). *A Stranger in My Own Body*. London: Karnac.

Fausto-Sterling, A. (2000). *Sexing the Body. Gender Politics and the Construction of Sexuality*. New York: Basic Books.

Foucault M. (1978) (ed.). *Herculine Barbin dite Alexina B.* Paris: Gallimard. [*Herculine Barbin: being the recently discovered memoirs of a nineteenth-century French hermaphrodite*, introduced by Michel Foucault. Translated by McDougall, R. New York, Pantheon Books, 1980].

Freud S. (1933a). *New Introductory Lectures on Psycho-Analysis*. (Lecture 33: "Femininity"). Standard Edition, **22**, 112–135

Geschwind, N. and Galaburda, A. (1987). *Cerebral Lateralization*. Oxford: Clarendon Press.

Godelier, M. (1982). *La production des Grands Hommes. Pouvoir et domination masculine chez les Baruya de Nouvelle-Guinée*, Paris, Fayard. *The Making of Great Men: male domination and power among the New Guinea Baruya*. Translated by Rupert Swyer, Cambridge [Cambridgeshire], New York, Cambrige University Press; and Paris, Editions de la Maison des Sciences de l'Homme, 1986.]

Goy, R. W., Berkovitch, F. B., and McBrair, M. C. (1988). "Behavioral masculinization is independent of genital masculinization in prenatally androgenized female rhesus macaques". *Hormones and Behavior*, **22**, 552–571.

Green, A. (1999). "Genèse et situation des états limites". In Jacques, A. *et al.* (eds). *Les états limites, nouveau paradigme pour la psychanalyse*. Paris: Presses Universitaires de France.

Green, R. (1987). *The "Sissy Boy Syndrome" and the Development of Homosexuality*. New Haven and London: Yale University Press.

Hausman, B. (1995). *Changing Sex. Technology and the Idea of Gender*. Durham, N.C.: Duke University Press.

Héritier, F. (2002). *Masculin/Féminin II: Dissoudre la Hiérarchie*. Paris: Odile Jacob.

Lévi-Strauss, C. (1973). "Réflexions sur l'atome de parenté". In *Anthropologie structurale deux*. Paris, Plon, 103–135. ["Reflections on the atom of kinship". In Lévi-Strauss, C. *Structural Anthropology*. Chicago: University of Chicago Press, vol. 2, pp. 82–112 (1976)].

Levine, S. and Shumaker, R. (1983). "Increasingly Ruth: toward understanding sex reassignment". *Archives of Sexual Behavior*. **12**, n°3, 247–61.

Lézine, I., Robin, M. and Cortial, C. (1975). "Observations sur le couple mère-enfant au cours des premières expériences alimentaires". *La Psychiatrie de l'Enfant*, 18, 1, 75–147.

Limentani, A. (1979). "The Significance of Transsexualism in Relation to Some Basic Psychoanalytic Concepts". *International Review of Psycho-Analysis*, **6**, 139–153.

Maccoby, E. and Jacklin, C. (1974). *The Psychology of Sex Differences*. Stanford: Stanford University Press.

McDougall, J. (1973). "L'idéal hermaphrodite et ses avatars". *Nouvelle Revue de Psychanalyse*, 7. Reprinted (1978) as "Hermaphrodite et la masturbation", in *Plaidoyer pour une certaine anormalité*. Paris: Gallimard [translated as "Masturbation and the Hermaphroditic Ideal", in (1980) *Plea for a Measure of Abnormality*. New York: International Universities Press. (2nd edition 1990: London: Brunner/Mazel)].

Mead, M. (1948). *Male and Female: A Study of the Sexes in a Changing World*. New York: William Morrow and Co.

Moberly, E. R. (1983). *Psychogenesis: The Early Development of Gender Identity*. London: Routledge & Kegan Paul.

Ovesey, L. and Person, E. (1973)."Gender Identity and Sexual Psychopathology in men: A Psychodynamic Analysis of Homosexuality, Transsexualism, and Transvestism". *Journal of the American Academy of Psychoanalysis*, **1**, 1, 53–72.

Rajon, A.-M. (1988)."La naissance de l'identité dans le cas des ambiguités sexuelles". *La Psychiatrie de l'Enfant*, **41**, 1, 5–35.

Richards, R. (1983). *Second Serve*. New York: Stein and Day.

Roiphe, H. and Galenson, E. (1981). *Infantile Origins of Sexual Identity*. New York: International Universities Press.

Salas, D. (1994). *Sujet de chair et sujet de droit: la justice face au transsexualisme*. Paris: Presses Universitaires de France.

Schaeffer, J. (1997). *Le Refus du Féminin*. Paris: Presses Universitaires de France.

Sésé-Léger, S. (1997). "Du désir de changement de sexe à la métamorphose subjective". In Chiland, C. (ed.). Approche psychothérapique du transsexualisme. *Perspectives psy*, **36**, 4, 285–289.

Stoller, R. J. (1968). *Sex and Gender*. vol. 1. New York: Science House.

— (1974). *Splitting. A case of female masculinity*. New York: Quadrangle; London: Hogarth.

— (1975). *Sex and Gender*. vol 2: *The Transsexual Experiment*. London: The Hogarth Press.

— (1985). *Presentations of Gender*. New Haven and London: Yale University Press.

Winnicott, D. W. (1965). "The effect of psychotic parents on the emotional development of the child". In *The Family and Individual Development*. London: Tavistock Publications.

Zhou J.-N., Hofman M. A., Gooren L. J. G., and Swaab D. F. (1995), A sex difference in the human brain and its relation to transsexuality, *Nature*, **377**, n° 6552, 68–70.

Index